Making the Light Come

Making the Light Come

THE POETRY OF

Gerald Stern

JANE SOMERVILLE

 Wayne State University Press   Detroit   1990

Library of Congress Cataloging-in-Publication Data
Somerville, Jane, 1934–
Making the light come : the poetry of Gerald Stern /
Jane Somerville.
p.   cm.
Includes bibliographical references.
ISBN 0–8143–2238–7 (alk. paper)
1. Stern, Gerald, 1925–   —Criticism and interpretation.
I. Title.
PS3569.T3888Z87   1990
811'.54—dc20   89–70498   CIP

Contents

Preface

Gerald Stern is a poet whose prominence has come late. His contemporaries won acclaim in the 1950s, as the lines were drawn between conservative and revolutionary elements in American poetry. Poets rose to prominence on both sides of the schism between academic formalism and the anti-establishment. Allen Ginsberg became a public symbol of the new poetry through the censorship trials that accompanied publication of *Howl* in 1956. On the other side of the controversy were traditional poets such as John Hollander, whose *A Crackling of Thorns* was chosen for the Yale Series of Younger Poets in 1958. That poets as opposed as these could win acclaim simultaneously illustrates the polarizing tendency of the time. This tendency, of course, is not an isolated one; the inclination to pursue extreme rhetorical positions typifies twentieth-century art as a whole and has led to such phenomena as the one-word poem and the white-on-white painting.

Stern did not participate in the upheaval that led many of his generation into extreme positions. He was born in 1925, a year earlier than Ginsberg and four years earlier than Hollander. He was actually a classmate of Ginsberg at Columbia, where he received the M.A. in 1949. Yet he did not begin to publish seriously until the late sixties. His first recognition came two decades after *Howl*, when in 1977, at the age of fifty-two, he won the Lamont Poetry Prize for *Lucky Life*. His place as an onlooker during the factious debates among poets of the fifties and sixties is a significant element in his

7

destiny. He was not hedged in as a defender of one position or another, a kind of commitment that can be hard to move beyond, as seen in the subsequent careers of Ginsberg and Hollander. Free of allegiances, Stern was able to draw on the resources of both tradition and revolution. Yet his poetry is not a middle-ground compromise of these extremes; instead, it is traditional and revolutionary at the same time: steeped in learnedness and respect for the past, yet possessed of anarchic vigor; obscure and allusive, yet conversational and direct.

Stern has a large and growing public, yet he has not yet attracted the critical attention called for by his important and complex work. This is partly because of his late arrival. It is also because he is not associated with a group such as the traditional, confessional, deep image, or language poets, and therefore his work is not included in discussions of particular strands of poetry. My goal is to provide an introduction that can serve as a basis for further discourse.

My primary obligation is to the poems themselves. It would be out-of-place to enter into a lengthy treatment of Stern's biography, his predecessors, philosophical sources, or relationships with contemporaries while the work itself remains to be examined. However, I have not hesitated to point toward such matters in passing when they help to explain the poems. And I have taken a particular interest in the impact of biblical materials on Stern, an influence I see as central. But my intent has been to subordinate secondary issues to interpretation of a body of work that is far more intricate and multifaceted than it seems at first reading. Dense and ambiguous, the Stern text is capable of responding to a wide range of discourse. The emphasis I have chosen and the *intercursus* it has prompted are but one avenue among many that invite attention.

I have organized my analysis in terms of the roles played by Stern's eccentric speaker, a voice and character which I see as the controlling principle in a poetry of performance. The first chapter is introductory. Here I delineate the function of the speaker against a brief biographical background, an approach to the issue of precursors, and a preliminary look at Stern's relationships with several poetic modes. I go on to suggest the tragi-comic as a generic position for the speaker and the poetry he controls. The second chapter treats nostalgia, the return journey which, more than a theme, is the underlying, engendering impulse throughout the canon, providing a corridor to transcendence. In the three remaining chapters, I take up the elemental roles enacted by the speaker: the figure of the gardener; the contrasting performances of the wanderer and the rabbi; and the angel, a presiding intermediary in the corpus.

I have taken this thematic approach with some reservations, since, even more than a poem-by-poem treatment, it interrupts the integrity of the poems. The critical act is definitively, of course, an intervention. Quoting parts of poems inevitably misrepresents them. Exposition follows a line which overemphasizes some points while excluding others, imposing its own order on what may be intentional ambiguity. In particular, the critic is led by his vocation to pass over those elements which resist interpretation. But the usefulness of a thematic approach outweighs all this in the case of Stern, since only by pulling up certain threads can the intricate crossweavings of the canon be made visible. It is a performative body of work that endlessly comments on itself, pointing back and forth from poem to poem in a continual interplay of shifting, overlapping, dissolving, and recurring motifs.

My view of the goals of criticism is somewhat old-fashioned. For me, criticism has to do with interpretation and also with appreciation. It should be useful to readers and, like any piece of writing, it should be pleasing in itself. The use of poetry to illustrate theory seems to me an odd enterprise, since theory is meant—or once was intended—as a tool for explaining poetry. The retreat into theory, it seems to me, is at least as problematic as was the old retreat into biographical and social comment. And no theory can, of course, explain greatness.

I have therefore made no effort to make this study the function of a theoretical stance, though I have made reference to theory here and there, to see what it may have to say about the work. I have tried instead to write a work of practical criticism which will be useful to readers. I have tried to align myself emotionally and intellectually with the poems, to engage in a sensuous appreciation of the text that is also scrupulous and attentive.

I am grateful to Gerald Stern for the time and attention he has given so generously to discussions of backgrounds in his work. I am grateful also to Fred Moramarco for reading the manuscript and providing a valuable commentary. I want to express appreciation to my mother, Kathryn Davis, for help and support throughout the course of this work. Thanks are due to the *American Poetry Review* for permission to reprint two chapters that appeared there and to

Poetry East for permission to reprint material from an essay published there. Finally, I would like to recognize the National Endowment for the Humanities, which provided a grant for a summer seminar during which this work was begun.

Acknowledgments

Excerpts from *Lovesick* by Gerald Stern, copyright © 1987 by Gerald Stern, are reprinted by permission of Harper & Row, Publishers, Inc. Poems quoted from *Rejoicings, Poems: 1966–1972* (1984) by Gerald Stern are reprinted by permission of Metro Book Co., 3208 Cahuenga Blvd. West, Los Angeles, CA 90068. Grateful acknowledgment is made to the following for permission to reprint from other works of Gerald Stern: Random House, Inc., for *Paradise Poems* (1984), copyright © 1984 Random House; and the *Journal of the Rutgers University Library* (1969), for "The Pineys."

Acknowledgment is also due to the following journals and books, where quoted works by Gerald Stern originally appeared: the *American Poetry Review* (1983–87), the *Paris Review* (1982), *Poetry East* (1986), *AWP Newsletter* (1987), *Poesis* (1984); *Lucky Life* (1977) and *The Red Coal* (1981), published by Houghton Mifflin; *45 Contemporary Poems* (1985), published by Longman; and *What Is a Poet?* (1987), edited by Hank Lazar, published by the University of Alabama Press.

➤ I ←

A Flowering Figure

The poetry of Gerald Stern is defined and governed by its flamboyant speaker, a stagey hero whose life story is the poet's, but enlarged and mythicized. This eloquent spokesman holds the line between the unconditional authority of narration and the contingency of character; in these we recognize the two positions we constantly hold as speakers and actors. He is onstage through the entire canon and constantly demands our attention. He does not react passively to events; he wrestles with them and shapes, even invents, the world he moves in. This invented realm is unstable and fortuitous, yet the Stern speaker is at ease in it and confident about its possibilities. He transforms himself endlessly, playing whatever parts appeal to him, yet his identity never changes: whether he takes the mask of a friendly gardener, a wandering hero, a rabbinical figure, a fallen angel, a god—even a tree or bird—he is still the same whimsical guy, a fantastic prophet and favorite uncle who, though full of wisdom, permits himself all manner of weakness, readily admits to his own foolishness, indulges in spates of sentiment, suffers endlessly, and overcomes suffering through imagination. In the gap between his vast proportions and his foolishness we recognize the human condition; in his capacity for transformation he becomes a metaphor for imagination.

This first-person narrator can of course be taken for the poet himself. But I prefer to see him as an actor, playing a part like that of a character in fiction who is said to "represent" the author. The distinction is subtle, but crucial. This view encourages us to notice the performative nature of Stern's poems. By focusing on the roles encapsulated in the protean speaker, we gain a framework in which to examine the complexities of the canon. This view also helps us to probe the distinction between the speaker and Stern himself.

Stern's leading character does seem to create an impression somewhat different from that of the typical lyric speaker. We are likely to think of the lyric speaker as sheer voice, as statement devised through certain strategies, in traditional or open form, in tone serious or ironic, in language plain or ornate. Identification tends to be scenic rather than dramatic. We seldom *picture* a lyric speaker or identify with him as a dramatic character, a "someone" who seems to be physically present and even seems to have an existence beyond the work, as do some characters in fiction: Huckleberry Finn, for instance, or Gatsby, or the Consul in *Under the Volcano*. Such a fictional character seems to have a material existence; he dominates the work he's in to such an extent that his entire world seems a function of himself. The meaning of the work is his meaning and cannot be separated from him; in this sense he is meaning itself. It is something of this quality, which combines independence, control, and irreducible meaning, that the Stern speaker conveys.

There are a number of other poets' narrators or characters who share, in some measure, a similar kind of dramatic status or, to put it another way, encourage the reader to invent a "living" character. The persona of Robert Frost is an example of a characterization which maintains a certain consistency through an entire canon, as does the Stern speaker. But the country philosopher we imagine in Frost is a type, not an individual, a function of setting and of the kinds of experience recounted rather than the idiosyncrasies of a unique personality. We can also compare Stern's narrator with single poems and poem cycles based on character. One thinks, for instance, of Hugh Selwyn Mauberley, J. Alfred Prufrock, and the Henry of John Berryman's *Dream Songs*. These seem, however, to be comparatively abstract. That is, they represent attitudes toward experience; they are characters—sets of values, moral positions, beliefs, and stances—more than personalities. These three also differ from Stern's speaker in that they are anti-heroic characters controlled by circumstance. Mauberley is a caricature, hardly visible; his most specifying feature is his name. He's an anti-self, while Stern's speaker is an ultraself. Prufrock is more picturable; he has a

13

certain jaunty air not unlike the Stern speaker, in spite of his ineffectuality. But we see him as a small fellow, not a grand figure. Berryman's Henry is like the Stern narrator in that he's a shape-shifter. But he has few picturable habits, and I doubt that readers imagine him as a "real guy." A stronger comparison than any of these is with *Leaves of Grass*; the Whitman persona is an imperative figure, magnified, heroized, and mythicized, as is Stern's spokes-man. Both are flashy exhibitionists; both are models of success rather than failure, of ultimate confidence rather than overriding doubt. But Whitman's character is played straight, while Stern's is not. The Stern speaker is comic as well as grand; his heroics are undermined by irreverence, irony, and jestful self-mockery.

The dramatic significance of Stern's speaker is in part a function of sheer presence: his high visibility through the whole course of the work gives the canon a novelistic consistency. Beyond this, significance coheres in the character himself, in a blend of elements that add up to a strong sense of *dasein*, agency, and confidence. For one thing, he is odd, quirky, conspicuous. He presents a striking combination of opposites: he is wild yet homey, heroic but clumsy, extreme yet down to earth, intimate yet distant. His lyricism is so overextended that it doubles back on itelf, becoming unlyrical. His verbal audacity is surprising, especially when compared with the safe, dull humming that characterizes so much of today's poetry. Our most audacious and startling work is that of the language poets, who, inspired by structuralist theory, surprise by trying to deny their own presence in the poem and indeed to deny the purpose of language itelf, which is not just to say but to say *something*. Stern's surprise rests on the opposite assertion, a cocky, half-kidding, rowdy display of idiosyncrasy and a conviction that there is still something to be said about the oldest subjects. Not since Stevens has there been a voice so quirky and original yet large and universal. Stevens, too, used his peculiar voice to reinvigorate classic themes.

Surprise for its own sake is of questionable merit. But the Stern speaker doesn't seem to be straining for effect; he appears really to *be that way*. At least, he does for many readers; to accept Stern on his own terms, the reader must be willing to identify with this character as an authentic voice. If he does not, he may prefer those poems where the speaker is least himself. Louis Simpson exemplifies this kind of reading. In a review of *Lovesick*, he faults

the poet for oversentimentality and strained emotion, which be-
comes "a performance." In short poems, he says, Stern "can be very
likable" (158–59). However, the longer poem is Stern's métier, pre-
cisely because it provides breathing space for the extremity of his
speaker.

The extremity and individuality of the speaker actually enhance
his authenticity: we tend to believe that he's sincere because he is so
recognizable and distinctive. We are also convinced by his vigor,
another quality that is unusual today, among so many slack, atten-
uated voices. His strength and authenticity rely on one another and
are induced by a combination of frank emotion, sincere yet idiosyn-
cratic speech, mixed tone, intimate voice, hyperactive syntax, and
largesse. All these are qualities not of a statement alone but of a
person, a character we accept as honest because of his oddity, his
boldness, his warmth, his admitted weakness, and his robust
confidence. We accept him also because he answers a need for
strength and authenticity and brings it in a form we can accept; he is
not the severe, commanding patriarch but the good father or
comforting uncle.

The distinction between this invention and the poet himself is a
simplistic and literal one: the speaker is not Gerald Stern because
the poet does not do, in real life, what the speaker does, and the
things that happen to the speaker don't literally happen to Stern.
The life events from which the poems spring are transformed in a
manner much more extreme than the usual change when a poet's
life becomes a semantic entity. The real Gerald Stern goes down to
the store to get a loaf of bread; the speaker embarks on a fabular
quest which leaves the loaf of bread behind, which overwhelms,
buries, or destroys mundane reality.

Another poet would invest the actual trip to the grocery with
significance. Stern's poem rarely insists that Gerald Stern's
wanderings on the city streets, his well-known restaurant stops, his
backyard gardening, or his travels abroad have, in themselves,
universal significance. Actual events in the poet's life often become
mere vestiges in the enlarged experience of the poem. The
distinction between the autobiographical Stern and his spokesman
is more extreme in some poems than in others. In his major work,
he escapes the limitations of biography through self-mythicization:
he invents an ultraself which shares his biography but is able to
enact a range of mythic roles. In fact, his entire poetic realm is

enveloped by the speaker. The people—even the plants and animals—have the stamp of his personality, which is that of Gerald Stern, but magnified: the corpus is an anthropomorphic universe full of this multiplied presence. The ultraself is at once self-magnifying and self-effacing, egocentric yet possessed of a certain humility which says, "It is not my particular circumstances that warrant attention; I am not a hero in myself but as a representative of human nobility." The hazard is the risk of *hubris,* acknowledged and countered in Stern's self-deflating foolishness and clumsiness.

In the most literal and obvious sense, it is not the poet who constantly changes form, but his creature: Gerald Stern does not become a tree, a squirrel, or a god. Transformation permits the poet to look at things from a range of extreme perspectives. It lets him experience himself as if he were another; he is able to explore possibilities not of the self alone but of the human. And it provides the opportunity to put himself at risk imaginatively. Transformation is perilous; it always implies the fear of disappearing. But the Stern speaker absorbs the threatening aspects of transformation in gallant confidence. He depicts his potential for regeneration and fruition by describing himself as "a flowering figure" (*PP* 61).[1] His capacity for transformation is the crux of Stern, the machinery of the poem and also its goal.

The oddity and authority of this spokesman derive in part from Stern's early isolation, his late development as a poet, and his lack of quick success. Born in 1925, he grew up in what he has called "inhospitable and merciless Pittsburgh," registered at the University of Pittsburgh almost by accident, was not even an English major:

> The idea of going to a school and studying under a poet never occurred to me. I didn't know yet who the poets were, and later, when I did, I had no idea where they worked—or that they did work. . . . I lived and studied without direction, and if anything was going to be a permanent influence on me it was that. ("Some Secrets" 258–60)

Through his private study, Stern "pieced together the story of modern poetry." But he did not attach himself to a dominant precursor. He says he did not have "one great influence, one master, but a number, even an endless number. . . ." Among them were Yeats and Auden in the mid-forties, Pound and early Eliot by the late forties, MacLeish, Cummings, Crane, Auden, Marlowe, Thomas, and Dickinson in the early fifties. By the mid-fifties, he was "most involved with Wallace Stevens." Lowell was "useful," but early Roethke was more so, because of "the mystery, the strangeness, the loss, the love of small animals and plants, the sense of justice." Williams was important for the way he combined "health and madness, domesticity and wildness" ("Some Secrets" 256–62; Glaser 10). In Emerson, Stern found a source for the poet's role in "the very making of the American vision," though he obviously disputes Emerson's rejection of tradition ("What Is This Poet?" 153). He has also identified any number of more distant sources; for instance, in a lengthy poetic tribute he takes Ovid's "books of sorrow" as a model (*PP* 21).

Among these diverse backgrounds are several that seem central in one way or another when the reader focuses on them, but in every case the distinctions are as serious as the similarities. For instance, a chapter could be devoted to Stern's relationship with early Eliot, in terms of specific elements such as reverence for tradition; incorporation of historic, philosophical, and literary allusions; mythicized place; narrative instability; and use of multiple voices. But in the largest sense, Stern has little in common with Eliot. He doesn't assent in Eliot's aristocratic hauteur, with its rejection of the vulgar present. His overall manner and his goals are quite different.

Pound, too, is clearly an important assimilation for Stern, though some characteristic Poundian features, such as interpolation of diverse times and cultures, derive from both Pound and Eliot. Pound's ideal of sincerity, defined in an image of the poet as one who has mastered both will and intellect, no doubt struck a responsive chord in Stern. However, volition in Stern is a continual assertion, an enterprise rather than a *fait accompli*. More crucial for Stern is the impact of the moments of illumination in the *Cantos*.

The most obvious, overriding, and frequently noticed source for Stern is Whitman. Yet Stern is irritated by the tendency of reviewers to make this comparison. He says he's "a Whitmanian who doesn't like to be called a Whitmanian." He recognizes his "obsession against the very idea of having someone as a teacher or guide." Though he admits to similarities in style and finds much to admire in "Song of Myself," he dislikes Whitman's "pat optimism," "chest-thumping," "shrill voice," and—most of all—his "preaching" (Glaser 11; "Some Secrets" 265; "What Is This Poet?" 153). Needless

17

to say, Harold Bloom would call this denial of Whitman a repression of the precursor. Perhaps Peter Stitt does go too far when he calls Stern "almost a spiritual reincarnation of Whitman" (880), but there are strong ties in attitude as well as manner. However, this influence is joined with others, in particular with that of Stevens. The odd conjunction of Stevensian gaudiness and intricacy with Whitmanian openness and emotionality is one of the sources of Stern's tensile strength. Various opposed and diverse influents have a tendency to disappear in the Stern poem, which is not a mixture but a compound that can't be reduced to its elements.

Stern does not see himself as "accountable," except in very obvious ways, to apparent influences. He is less inclined to identify literary antecedents than aspects of his "personal, accidental history," such as Judaism, the depression, the political left, the crucial childhood loss of his sister—even being left-handed. Ultimately, he believes his own loss and failure became his subject ("Some Secrets" 256–57, 263). In a sense, his failed self became the master he had to vanquish.

He says he knows nothing about "the psychology of masterhood" ("Some Secrets" 258). It may have been "a certain shyness and a certain secrecy, coupled with a kind of arrogance" that made him "unwilling to submit," to become a protegé like Lowell of Tate or "Allen Ginsberg on W.C.W.'s side porch, or Pound in the Provençal room or Whitman in the Emerson room. . . ." He did make one attempt to connect with the poetry establishment. He showed an early, epic poem called "Ishmael's Dream" to Auden, and was ignored ("Some Secrets" 256, 261). "In Memory of W. H. Auden" (*PP* 9) reimagines this crucial rejection without explaining what happened:

> it was cold and brutal outside on Fourth Street
> as I walked back to the Seventh Avenue subway,
> knowing, as I reached the crowded stairway,
> that I would have to wait for ten more years
> or maybe twenty more years for the first riches
> to come my way, and knowing that the stick
> of that old Prospero would never rest
> on my poor head, dear as he was with his robes
> and his books of magic, good and wise as he was
> in his wrinkled suit and his battered slippers.

The poem is a coming-to-terms wherein the poet pictures himself "waving goodbye" to "that magician / who could release me now, whom I release and remember."

In another poem, Stern describes what it was like to be an outsider, to hope he wouldn't always be "out there" with only his odd thoughts and his own speech, his "lips alone," to guide him:

> hoping I don't have to spend the rest of my life out there
> staring through the trees,
> hoping that my odd mind will keep me going
> if nothing else does
> and hoping my lips alone can carry me from place to place
> and tremble when they have to, and sing when they have to,
> without help, or interference. (*LL* 30)

He came to see himself as "staking out a place that no one else wanted because it was abandoned or overlooked" ("Some Secrets" 264). Clearly he was aware that he was writing against the grain. His determination to be self-originating, while it stems in part from failure, can be seen as a signal of the strong poet.

The only overarching background for his work, in terms of style and in a much broader sense, is biblical literature, in particular the kabbalistic and Hassidic reinterpretations of Talmud and the Midrashim. He puts these to his own uses ("Some Secrets" 257). In fact, the major roles played by his speaker are appropriations of biblical figures and concepts, as I will demonstrate in later chapters. Implicit in his thought is a usurped or reconstituted concept of Jesus which replaces the typical, Christian image. Thus the Bible—and more importantly the commentaries that readjust and even reverse biblical material—can be taken as his precursor.

In 1958, Stern began work on a book-length poem called "The Pineys," which was published in 1969 in the *Journal of the Rutgers University Library*. A treatise on the people of a southern New Jersey wilderness known as the Pine Barrens, the poem illustrates the experimentation that preceded Stern's realized style.[2] Some parts are written in rather strict iambic pentameter, with formal diction; at its worst, it sounds clogged and pretentious:

19

in the one place hylic, in the next
A limp platonic; stony luminous; heartless;
Each a plighting, a plashing, on the ripe occasion,
A raging, of those that rage, and less of it those
That rage less, all with their own inculpable quavers, ("Pineys" 58)

Two sections play on the relationship between metaphors and algebraic formulas, or poetry and logic; they bristle with lines like these: "And x prevailed only, and always, as z, / As opposed to y, which would be the state without z . . ." (66). Another part consists of a list of 298 numbered items defining "what the starved and beaten Pineys were symbols of . . ." (67–71). The segment dealing with the actual history of the Pineys (part two) is spoken in a voice closer to the one we know in later Stern. There are hints of this voice throughout the mélange of the poem; it also contains many of Stern's themes and displays the tragi-comic flavor that will later be invested in his speaker.

After completing "The Pineys," Stern underwent a *crise de quarante*: "I realized the poem was a failure. . . . I had been a practicing poet for almost two decades and I had nothing to show. . . . I had reached the bottom." His failure became a liberation: "I was able to let go and finally become myself and lose my shame and my pride." His work changed suddenly, "as if I had been preparing for this all my life . . . and now I was ready" ("Some Secrets" 262–64). He abandoned formal rhythms and high-flown diction. He relinquished spatiotemporal coherence. He gave up adherence to a comprehensible literal situation in the poem. He began to rely on an idiosyncratic speaker, a voice and personage that would be himself-in-art.

A new Stern poem emerges in *Rejoicings*, published in 1973.[3] The book got little notice, but it contains several important poems and announces virtually all of Stern's themes and motifs as well as key words and images. His stubborn refusal to follow the rules is also in evidence: unsuppressed emotion, sentimentality, classical allusion, the flaunting of abstractions, the unpopular happy outlook suggested somewhat fallaciously by his titles—all these go against the dogma of poetry writing that has been dominant for decades in the classroom and beyond. Yet he has clung persistently, in the decades since *Rejoicings*, to his aberrations. If he gets by with all this, it is not because the complex ambivalences of his work have been taken into account. The credit goes to his speaker, who is already clearly defined in *Rejoicings*, though he is not so consistently at ease as he will be later and sometimes veers off into silliness. The few poems from which he is absent, such as "Goodbye, Morbid Bear," "No Succour!" and "The Heat Rises in Gusts," demonstrate how crucial he is to Stern's originality. In the weakest of these, "Two American Haikus," drops of rain fall "like heads / dropping into the waste basket" (*R* 60). Without the mediation of the speaker, this surreal image seems lifted from a film by Jean Cocteau or Maya Deren.

It was not until *Lucky Life*, which won the Lamont Poetry Prize for 1977, that Stern began to succeed; he was fifty-two years old. He later came to value the years of alienation, to believe, as he says in a poem from *The Red Coal*, that "nothing was wasted, that the freezing nights / were not a waste, that the long dull walks and / the boredom, and the secret pity, were / not a waste" (*RC* 71). He believes that his poetry resulted from his isolation: "I went where I did go because I didn't have a guide and I became what I am for that reason . . ." ("Some Secrets" 265).

By *Lucky Life*, most of the fumblings and inconsistencies visible in *Rejoicings* have gone. Stern is already, with his first widely received book, in the mature period of his work; the radical shifts we often observe in the early part of a poet's career have passed without notice. The eccentricity and strength that grow in isolation are portrayed through the speaker, who can almost be called a stand-in for the master Stern lacked, an Adamic offshoot of his own will made to rule in his invented realm.

When the Stern speaker first appeared in *Rejoicings*, the poetry schools of the fifties, reactions against academicized modernism, were a decade old. Ginsberg, born only a year after Stern, had long since challenged the academy. Stern remembers his reaction to "beat vs. feet" as ambiguous: he cursed the academics, "with their wit and elegance and politeness and forms," yet he could not accept the anti intellectual posture of the poetic left or its lack of imagination ("Some Secrets" 260–62). His speaker is, on one level, an attempt to reconcile the extremes of intellect and emotion, mind and body. His reverence for learnedness is a strong presence throughout the corpus, but his respect for the physical/emotional is just as serious, as he says in a poem where the squirrel represents body and feeling:

21

I need a squirrel,
his clawed feet spread, his whole soul quivering,
the hot wind rushing through his hair,
the loud noise shaking him from head to tail.

O philosphical mind, O mind of paper, I need a squirrel
finishing his wild dash across the highway,
rushing up his green ungoverned hillside.   (*RC* 23)

Throughout his career, Stern has never participated in the shared aesthetic of any cluster of poets; he cannot be placed in any school or group. But he does share common ground with various modes, and I hope to clarify his position through comparison. Needless to say, such comparisons are inherently sketchy and generic; they overlook the extreme differences between poets in any group, not to mention the differences within the canon of a single poet. My purpose is only to propose some similarities and distinctions between Stern and certain modes; I hope that this brief discussion will set the stage for closer comparisons.

Stern has something in common with both sides of a broad yet significant dichotomy in postmodern poetry between the sincere and the ironic. In the first case, he has similar goals but a different style; in the second his style is similar but his goals are quite distinct.

The sincere poem, or the "scenic style," as Altieri calls it, blurs into the "deep image poem" and is seen in major poets as different as Kunitz, Merwin, Stafford, and Bly. It is often said to be the dominant mode of recent decades. It presents a resolutely quotidian world invested in some cases with surreal and archetypal significance. It is serious, direct, and unaffected, quietly emotional, often passive. Paul Hoover labels it "moral poetry." Its chief ingredients, he says, are ecstasy and grief, its role prophetic (14). At its best, it achieves a severe clairvoyance. At its worst, it takes itself too seriously. Stern shares the ecstatic and grieving postures of this mode and its impulse toward prophecy, but in an opposite style. His speaker is much too flamboyant and comic a fellow—and too much a trickster—to appear in the sincere poem. And the adventures of this speaker are anything but quotidian. They range out into history:

A Flowering Figure

I am in a certain century again
going from city to city. I am in a window
with Berlioz on my left and Czerny on my right;
Liszt is looking into the clouds, his wrists
seem to be waiting. . . .   (L 10)

His adventures also become mythic, enlarged by ancestral memory: "Always I am in the middle of everything. / My voice is in the woods; / my hands are in the water; / my face is in the clouds, like a hot sun" (RC 7).

The ironic poem has aristocratic roots; it is seen in the New York School and epitomized by John Ashbery. We think of it as witty, subtle, and cool. Stern's ardent humanism seems quite at odds with its brittle, disconnected posture, though his respect for high culture and intellect can be called aristocratic. Stylistically, Stern has much in common with Ashbery: a whimsical air, playfulness, elision, a combination of abstractness and conversational directness, accessible moments dissolved in convoluted syntax, rejection of logic, invention of an alternative realm. Stern is more emotional, Ashbery more detached. The surface similarities between these poets tend to go unnoticed because they are so different at heart. Ashbery's stance toward meaning is definitively ironic in its rejection of wholeness, but Stern's is not. Stern's irony is occasional, soft, often hidden and ambivalent. The Stern speaker is wildly sincere; at the same time, he smiles at the irony of his own seriousness, recognizing the finitude of his experience. Stern has remarked on his attitude toward irony versus seriousness:

. . . though I love irony and playfulness and roles and symbolic behavior and indirect action and irony itself (and lying and concealing and masquerie and buffoonerie)—at bottom I believe my life and the life of the universe is deeply serious, even unforgettable. ("Life Is Not a River" 9)

Overriding irony doesn't suit Stern, because it denies the reconciliation of real and ideal which is one of his goals. Occasional, playful irony, however, is a way out of the impasse that irony creates; it is a way of being ironic and naive at almost the same time. It avoids both the self-absorption of romantic irony, which aims to distance and reverse alienation, and the pretensions of hand-over-heart seriousness.

Stern is most often associated with the accumulative or discursive poem that comes out of Whitman, through Ginsberg, and, in modified form, into poets like Robert Pinsky or Ed Dorn. His long, profuse lines, parallel structures, and digressive strategies identify him with this full kind of poem. The main difference here is a subtle distinction in subject and purpose. These poets are ordinarily thought of as representatives of American society or prophets of American experience. Stern can certainly be read in this vein, and reviewers often do so. However, he places American issues in distant and mythic contexts. He is concerned with explication of social realities, but his central goal rests on creating a certain kind of experience in the poem, which may be called the apprehension of archetypes.

In this he resembles the version of sincere poetry often called "deep image" or "archetypal." But he encounters the archetype as drama, not image; his impulse is verbal, not adjectival. He has noted his attraction to the deep image, which he says is central to all poetry, but not to the bare, minimal work that we think of in connection with deep image poets: "I want the poem to have resonance in several places at once. . . . I want it to be arduous, yet simple. . . . I don't want to say the 'gray gray' and let it go at that. I want to live in a number of worlds" (Hillringhouse 30). He accomplishes this multiform poem through his speaker, whose dramatized sensibility pulls in and unifies diverse elements.

Stern has a tangential relationship with the kind of poem we call confessional, a kind hard to discuss because it is not a style but an impulse that appears widely. Obviously, the confessional tendency of Lowell assumes a vastly different form from that of Berryman, Plath, or Bishop. Yet they all share an unprecedented overt expression of obsessive self-fascination. Historically, we can point to a reaction against modernist impersonality, a renewed, radicalized, and inward-facing romanticism wherein self-expression and emotionality focus not on the response of self to world but on the psychology of self. In the most general terms, we can speak of a poetry in which self-expression becomes self-exposure. We might go so far as to call the confessional poem an endgame of the self as subject. Stern questions the prevailing emphasis on the self in poetry as a whole; he posits a time when "perhaps the pain in the life of the poet will stop being the main subject . . ." ("Notes" 13.1: 19). Yet he sees the stress on self as an inevitable consequence of the fact that "we don't have a common history in this country, a common culture." It reflects "the fact that we're all separate from each other" (Glaser 27).

There's a surface resemblance between Stern's work and the confessional stance that turns out to be false. The Stern speaker displays himself flagrantly, almost shamelessly. We feel that we know not only his personality but his character; yet, like a person we see often around town, we know him from the outside in—not from the inside out. This is the opposite of our response to the psychological emphasis that typifies the confessional poem. At one point, Stern offers a half-mocking confession that may be taken partly as a joke on confessional poets and partly as a joke on himself:

> I ate my sandwich
> and waited for a signal, then I began
> my own confession; I walked on the stones, I sighed
> under a hemlock, I whistled under a pine,
> and reached my own house almost out of breath
> from walking too fast—from talking too loud—
> from waving my arms and beating my palms; I was,
> for five or ten minutes, one of those madmen you see
> forcing their way down Broadway, reasoning with themselves
> the way a squirrel does . . .   (L 23)

If there is a poet among the diverse group of confessionals with whom Stern has an affinity, it is Berryman. Both use a strained syntax, though Berryman's is jumpy while Stern's is evasive, so smooth and flowing that its transmutations tend to go unnoticed. More central is the relationship between Stern's multiplied speaker and Berryman's Henry, "a human American man" with many names who enacts a multiplicity of "sad wild riffs." Both are suffering yet comic. But Henry's world is diminished, etiolated, finally unredeemable; he sums it up when he says, "All human pleas / are headed for the night."

The concept of the confessional poem is undermined by the fact that the word itself is a misnomer. The word *confession* implies admission of guilt and need for forgiveness. The confessional poem, on the other hand, has strong roots in Freudian blame: "Look what they've done to me." Stern's poem is closer to the word *confess* than the misnamed confessional poem, because he makes a habit of pleading for forgiveness. He does so, often comically, throughout the corpus: "Please forgive me, my old friends" (*R* 40); "Forgive me ten times, but this is what I did" (*LL* 87); ". . . dreaming of my weaknesses / and praying to the ducks for forgiveness" (*RC* 64); "forgive me / for turning into a tree, forgive me, you lovers / of life for leaving you suddenly" (*PP* 61); "I sit in the sun forgiving myself" (*L* 52); "I have to be forgiven" (*L* 74). These entreaties sound like lighthearted, formal courtesies, yet they surely point to the unreasonable childhood guilt he felt at his sister's early death. If we want to take guilt as a psychological motive in the confessional poem, we can propose a similar possibility in Stern, though not as a crucial element.

A major distinction between Stern and the confessionals is one of tone. For one thing, the rage that typifies some of these poets, notably Plath and Sexton, is missing from his work. So is the overriding negativity which is not just an acknowledgment of suffering but an embrace of it, a sometimes potent one. If Lowell can say, at one point, "I myself am hell," Stern is more likely to see his projected self as the potential for paradise. Suffering is a central concept in Stern; however, it is the transformative suffering of the hero. And, like other "high" aspects of Stern's work, it is leavened by comedy.

Stern's acknowledged self-pity does seem to find an echo in confessional poetry, but here too there's a tonal difference. Confessional poets, though they sometimes seem absorbed by self-pity, don't state it directly. Stern, on the other hand, kids openly about it, acknowledging human weakness. At one point, the speaker is looking for his kidney along the road:

> I want to see it
> weeping with pure self-pity, wringing its hands
> the way a kidney wrings its hands, much better
> than the liver, much better than the heart . . . (*PP* 70)

In the largest sense, his self-pity is part of the encompassing tragic pity central in his work.

Stern shares the intense emotionality of the typical confessional poem, but not its frank disclosure. In Stern, sources of effusive feeling are often eclipsed. Crucial personal material is visible here and there: his early failure, the central incident of his sister's death, his relationship with his father. But the poem is never imprisoned by its fact. He never writes a poem about these subjects; references to them are immersed in historic, mythic, or fantastic encounters. Often, only an embedded nugget of the literal situation which instigated a poem is left in, as if one were to recall a passionate sexual interlude, for instance, or a scene of anguish, but write down only one or two details of the scene. At one point, he denies such hidden meaning:

> here is my yellow tablet, there are no
> magic thumb prints, nothing that is not there,
> only the hum, and I have buried that
> on the piece of paper. . . .   (*L* 40)

A few lines later, he almost takes back this denial when he says his words are made to be hidden away in a hip pocket or wallet, "and there are broken words, / or torn, hanging onto the threads, the deep ones / underneath the flap, the dark ones forever creased" (*L* 41). These "dark ones" may be remnants of private material; they also point to Stern's interest in mystical Judaism and in what he calls "the secret text" ("What Is This Poet?" 153). References to secrets appear throughout Stern. This stealthiness plays against the overt, passionate outbursts that mark the canon. The opposition between concealment and disclosure, inside and outside, subconscious and conscious, is one of many dualisms in Stern.

Secrecy is at odds with the whole religio-Freudian workings of confession, which requires laying bare of the most intimate problems—problems which may seem trivial or infantile when seen in the shadow of the killing grounds. It is also at odds with the postmodern preference for openness. A secretive poem is inaccessible and therefore undemocratic. Concealed meaning does have value, though: it creates a substratum which puts pressure on the poem's compressed surface; the surface is intensified beyond its apparent meaning, as ordinary events are intensified by hidden meanings in dreams.

Secrecy encourages the old-fashioned, formalist approach to reading, which may be called the quest reading: initial impenetrability or confusion, an engagement like wrestling with an angel, and final illumination. This reading style is out of favor because it traditionally looked for a single meaning supported by every aspect of the text. Stern's canon does not answer this demand for consistency. There are even irreducibles in the text whose presence must be accepted on their own terms, or on faith. But the quest reading can be used to open multiple possibilities. Formalism is out of favor also because it seems to value the poem's surface only for what it conceals. But in fact, the process itself, like any quest, is valuable. In Stern's case, the poem has an equally strong tendency to pull the reader in the other direction, away from interpretation, to keep her poised on the poem's gaudy surface.

Though we don't see a lot of private material in Stern, we are constantly looking at the speaker as he moves about on the stage of the poem and listening to his distinctive descriptions of his own actions. The speaker often says *I am here* or *here I am again*, insisting in present tense that we acknowledge the physicality of his presence. And as scene-setter, he often begins a poem with *this is*, asserting the actuality of the setting as well. His continual self-description creates the effect of dramatic presence. It works to establish the kind of sympathy or identification we give to a fictional character, not, on the surface at least, the kind demanded by confessional. Yet it cannot be denied that Stern's early need for recognition survives under the surface; the speaker says, in effect, here I am; please accept me. He wants to be seen; detailed descriptions of his movements and gestures as well as what he sees—or will see or might see—from his exact perspective serve to make him visible:

> In my left hand is a bottle of Tango.
> In my right hand are the old weeds and power lines.   (*R* 23)

> I can relax in the broken glass
> and the old pile of chair legs;   (*R* 32)

> I am so exhausted I can barely lift my arms over my head
>   to pull the vines down.   (*LL* 11)

> Today I am sitting outside the Dutch Castle
> on Route 30 near Bird in Hand and Blue Ball,   (*RC* 43)

> One arm I'll hold up in the snake position
> above my head
> and one arm I'll hold out like a hairy fox
> waiting to spring. . . .   (*PP* 7)

28

I bend my face and cock my head. My eyes
are open wide listening to the sound.
My hand goes up and down like a hummingbird.   (*PP* 15)

I hold my arm out straight like a dirty drunk,
I walk the plank between the rhododendron
and the little pear. . . .   (*PP* 44)

I'm eating breakfast even if it means standing
in front of the sink and tearing at the grapefruit,   (*L* 58)

     I bend my lips to the moon,
I wait for the tide, I touch myself with mud,
the forehead first, the armpits, behind the knees,
clothes or no clothes; now I walk on my face,
I had to do that, now I walk on the wires,
now I am on the moon . . .   (*L* 70)

As seen in these typical selections, gestural notations are present as early as *Rejoicings*. But they become more profuse and unusual later. They are never superficial. Themes and ideas are bound up in the very gestures of the speaker, as they are in the theater. For instance, the major theme of waste and ruin is embodied in the first two quotations above. These gestures seem irreducible; they insist on a collaboration between signifier and signified, a reunion of word and world. Structuralist thinking sometimes calls such union a romantic delusion, and so it is; it's the kind of belief we used to innocently hold about art. It is experienced, and therefore, though it can be dismissed in meta-discourse, it is true on its own level. It is in this sense that Stern's oddball character with his funny, often ritualized behavior is not just a speaker of meaning but meaning itself.

The confessional poem, in its self-absorbed focus on one life, tends to differentiate that life, to set it off from others, in spite of the fact that it may stand as an example. In Stern, on the other hand, the poet's experience is not the main subject of the work. Stern's invented self is, in spite of its oddness, a representative figure: the poet or the man. In Stern, it is not, finally, "look how I have suffered" but "look how we suffer." The underlying impulse is the longing to connect, to make oneself part of the whole—a need fostered in Stern by alienation. This movement toward union is an ancient function of literature, often lost in contemporary writing that is centered in the effort to separate, to distinguish between rather than unite.

The intimacy of confessional poetry led inevitably to a reaction against self-portrayal seen in the so-called persona poem, a recent mode where the subject—at least ostensibly—is a historical figure. In another, related reaction, private life is still the subject, but the poet disavows the *I*, distancing himself as a *he*, a *she*, or even a *you*. Stern's relationship to these kinds of poems is complicated.

In his predominant first-person poems, the Stern speaker often creates an impresssion like that of poems where the self is pushed into third person. The speaker makes himself an object of scrutiny: "I will look at my greenish eyes in the mirror / and touch my graying hair and twist my hat" (*LL* 35); "I study my red hand under the faucet, the left one" (*RC* 68). Stern's preoccupation with hands stems from his being left-handed, which labeled him early on as an alien, and also from biblical influence. Continual reference to right and left hands manifests the text's bipolar or dualistic nature. The two hands also have to do with two kinds of gesturing and two selves: the right is potent and magisterial, the left has implications of imperfection and insincerity. In the mirror, the speaker becomes whole, "a mirror right-hander, / not a crazy twisted left-handed cripple, / trying to live in this world . . . " (*L* 52). In this sense, the speaker is a reflected self, perfected in the mirror of the work. "I stare at myself," he says; "the trick is finally to do it / without a mirror" (*L* 80).

The closest Stern comes to the persona poem is "Father Guzman," a book-length dramatic piece which appeared in *Paris Review* but has not been collected. Here he gives up first person, focuses on fictional characters, and even sacrifices the evasions of narration. The priest Guzman and Boy, his ephebe, are self-projections who both sound much like Stern's first-person speaker, but they are on-stage without the convolutions of tense and syntax that mystify his usual appearance.

Stern often writes poems that are ostensibly about or addressed to historic figures, especially in *The Red Coal* and *Paradise Poems*: "Magritte Dancing" (*RC* 26–27), "Thinking about Shelley" (*RC* 34–35), "The Picasso Poem" (*RC* 80–81), "Villa-Lobos" (*PP* 57), "Kissing Stieglitz Goodbye" (*PP* 66–67), and others. But these are nominal or partial subjects, or taking-off points; the poems are really about the speaker's thoughts, and he oftens says so: "My mind is on Hobbes" (L 55); "I started . . . thinking about Shelley" (RC 34). When he praises Villa-Lobos or imagines Spinoza "saying something perfect and sweet and exact / as always" (PP 65), it sounds as if he's really talking about himself but wants to avoid self-aggrandizement. These can't really be called persona poems, since the speaker doesn't stay out of them.

In fact, he often gets right into the imagined scene. "Béla" (L 12–14), for instance, starts off as a "version" of Bartók composing his last concerto on his deathbed. In a typical Sternian double-scene, the speaker is also playing a record of the music. A rehearsal is pictured—or rather, the speaker recalls a photograph of a rehearsal—and the speaker begins to participate: "I lift / my own right hand, naturally I do that; / I listen to my blood, I touch my wrist." By the end of the poem, the speaker has forced his way into a sentence with Bartók's wife: "she waits in agony, / she goes to the telephone; I turn to the window, / I stare at my palm, I draw a heart in the dust, / I put the arrow through it, I place the letters / one inside the other." The I asserts his authority as controlling consciousness and maker of the poem, the one who "places the letters." He also asserts his right to make sentimental gestures.

In other poems, Stern merges with the subject figure in complex, nested scenarios. In "The Same Moon Above Us" (PP 19–22), the speaker sees a vagrant "sleeping over the grilles" and thinks "he must be Ovid dreaming / again of Rome." The I goes on to describe the thoughts of he, an Ovid metamorphosed on Prince Street "at the long bar / across the street from New York Kitchen." The bum becomes Ovid, Ovid becomes Stern, Stern assumes the role of the representative poet, all are distanced by the voice of the speaker, who is also Stern. In this typical pattern, it seems that the speaker absorbs various roles, rather than to change into them; all remain simultaneously present. At the end of the poem, the speaker leaves Ovid and finds himself "in the middle of nowhere," as Stern was in his early career, with no audience for his virtuoso performance: "no one to see / his gorgeous retrieval, no one to shake the air / with loud applause and no one to turn and bow to. . . ."

Another Sternian strategy that bears some resemblance to use of persona is his identification with a plant or animal. Sometimes he takes the form of a bird: "I am just that one pigeon / limping over towards that one sycamore tree / with my left leg swollen and my left claw bent" (*L* 31); "I move thoughtfully from branch to branch, / . . . I think of my own legs as breaking off / or my wings coming loose in the wind / or my blossoms dropping onto the ground" (*LL* 21). Here the speaker becomes a bird and then immediately merges with a blossoming tree.

The speaker usually winds into and out of these masks briefly and with such a display of legerdemain that he's hard to catch. In one atypical poem, the narrator throughout is a dead dog who waits for the "lover of dead things" to "come back / with his pencil sharpened and his piece of white paper" (*L* 34–35). He's waiting for Stern —that is, for the Stern speaker, who is seen in many poems with a stub of pencil and who often professes his love for dead things. The dog observes him: "his mouth is open and his glasses are slipping." The ironic relationship between the dog and this "great loving stranger" is like the one between an unfortunate and a tyrant—or between man and god. The dog hopes he won't be kicked aside; he cries for pity. He has traded his "wildness"; he waits for "the cookie," snaps his teeth "as you have taught me, oh distant and brilliant and lonely." Like all Stern's characters, the dog sounds like his master; he isn't a foil for the speaker but an extension of him. The poem isn't about the dog, it's about the man—or Man.

Stern's use of persona is more like that of the high moderns than that of the recent persona poem. A similar pantheon of shifting and merging personae is definitive in Joyce, Eliot, Stevens, and others. The conventional notion is that it stems from loss of identity and reflects the fragmented modern self. This rings true for Eliot and Joyce, where characters without strong boundaries merge into other characters and, as Leopold Bloom says, "noone is anything." It does not ring true for Stevens, where the personae are enchanting and heroic. And it does not ring true for Stern. We don't feel ennui in Stern, or absence of will. Instead, we sense an expansive self that swells to fill robustly all its presences, each of which is added to the possibilities for enactment of a willed destiny. In a Whitmanesque passage where the Stern speaker addresses himself—or perhaps addresses Gerald Stern—the *you* becomes everyone: ". . . you see yourself out there, you are a swimmer / in an old wool suit, you are an angry cabbie, / you are a jeweler, you are a whore . . ." (*L* 67). The passage continues in a tour de force chain of associations that levels and bonds virtually everything; metamorphosis in Stern is not division or separation but multiplication or connection. It stems from the dream of unity, of an unbroken chain: "when nothing is lost, when I can go forth and forth, / when the chain does not break off, that is paradise" (*L* 68).

Though Stern doesn't fit easily into any of the schools or groups of poets that have waxed and waned during his career, he can be placed in the broad, diffuse category of the neo-romantic: a modern or postmodern poet who shares certain motives of the romantics, not innocently but from a retrospective distance. Sanford Pinsker suggests the romantic label in a *Missouri Review* interview taped in 1979; he calls Stern "that rarest of creatures—a likable Romantic," and compounds his sins, as he says, by suggesting "Jewish Romantic" and "Semi-Urban Romantic." He points to Stern's "high intensities" and his "prophetic quality" (56, 59, 64–65). Many of the preferences we associate with textbook concepts of romanticism are evident in Stern: subjectivity, improbability, emotionality, spontaneity, the dynamic, the infinite. His boldness underlined by melancholy is typically romantic, as is his reverence for a natural world infused with feeling and spirit. The most obvious distinction between Stern and the broad concept of romanticism is the high value he places on history, civilization, and culture.

His relationship with nature—or the world—can be defined in traditional romantic terms as a reunion, or in the later view epitomized by Harold Bloom, where nature is usurped by imagination. Or it can be examined in relation to a more complex view of romanticism as the paradox of consciousness. This view is still most convincingly put by Robert Pinsky. He sees Keats's relationship with the nightingale as an approach-avoidance mechanism that regrets the burden of consciousness, yet recognizes that without it we do not exist (47–52). The paradox of consciousness and the effort to overcome it through willful imagination is portrayed in Stern as a romantic quandary conditioned by the modern. It is serious, but also ironic, comic, and ultimately tragic—in the classical, not the popular sense of that term. Tragedy is, in fact, the consequence of consciousness, the recognition of our nature and destiny.

Two distinctions between Stern's performance and the romantic plot combine to establish his genre: the comic and the tragic. Stern's own definition of tragi-comedy is "going through the motions of prayer without prayer."[4] He might have said "going through the *emotions* of prayer without an object of belief," a response to the modern dilemma which Stevens described by substituting the verb

believe for the noun *belief.* Modern tragedy always has comic under-
tones because it is heroism cut off from absolutes. The hero whose
tragic fall is not from some great height but from a curbstone is ludi-
crous; this is the basis of the absurd.

Stern's speaker-hero is a tragi-comic character whose closest rel-
atives can be found in drama and fiction rather than among the
poets. He sometimes calls to mind Chaplin's resourceful tramp, a
forerunner of the absurd hero, whose life is accidental yet hopeful.
His zany jeremiad comes closer to Beckett or Pinter, and even closer
to Saul Bellow's *Henderson the Rain King.*

Like those of the Stern speaker, Henderson's lavish adventures
are fabular and fantastic. Both characters have the same kind of
bizarre vitality. Both are rambling and impulsive. Both contain
charged opposites; they are pathetic and heroic, serious and ironic,
comic and godlike. Both are obsessed by suffering and transcen-
dence. And their voices are strikingly similar. Here's Henderson:

> The left hand shakes with the right hand, . . . the hands play
> patty-cake, and the feet dance with each other. And the sea-
> sons. And the stars, and all of that. (276)

> As he waited to achieve his heart's desire, he was telling me
> that suffering was the closest thing to worship that I knew any-
> thing about. . . . I *was* monstrously proud of my suffering. I
> thought there was nobody in the world that could suffer quite
> like me. (255)

Here's the Stern speaker, talking about himself:

> The truth is he has become his own sad poem,
> he walks and eats and sleeps in total sadness,
> sadness is even what he calls his life, he
> is the teacher of sadness . . .   (*PP* 20)

> and it is his own regret that moves him to tears
> and his own sorrow that saves him—he is saved
> by his own sorrow—it is his victory—   (*PP* 21)

> two great masters of suffering and sadness
> singing songs about love and regeneration.   (*PP* 18)

A Flowering Figure

The similarity between Stern and Bellow is partly a function of their similar responses to Jewish tradition. Jewish and biblical influence is apparent in the joyful sadness of both writers, in their language and phrasing, their emphasis on suffering, and their respect for tradition and learning. Rabbinical tendencies can be seen in both; in fact, the Stern speaker often assumes a rabbinical mask.

Behind all the masks and ruses of Stern's spokesman stands a single character who, like the traditional tragi-comic protagonist, is known for his passionate outbursts and the surprising turns of plot in which he is immersed. He also reminds us of the buffoon, an archetypal character defined by Susanne Langer as "the indomitable living creature fending for itself, tumbling and stumbling" like a clown, caught up in "absurd expectations and disappointments," living through "an improvised existence" (342). In spite of his chancy life, the Stern speaker is buoyant and hopeful. He creates an overarching conviction, but it is not a presiding fate. Instead it is a ruling faith that is neither smug nor rosy. It is uncertain and must be continually accomplished, yet we share the speaker's confidence that it will prevail.

Though his outlandish performance sometimes borders on burlesque, the Stern speaker enacts all the characteristics of the tragic hero. He sometimes becomes almost godlike; with overweening pride, he imagines himself as the creator: "I put the clouds in their place and start the ocean / on its daily journey up the sand . . . " (R 11). He crowns himself with the garland of the classical hero: "I make a garland for my head, it is / a garland of pity—I won't say glory . . . it is the terror" (L 33). The experience he embodies and creates is suffused with tragic terror and pity:

> pity is for this life, pity is the worm
> inside the meat, pity is the meat, pity
> is the shaking pencil, pity is the shaking voice—
> not enough money, not enough love—pity
> for all of us—it is our grace, walking
> down the ramp or on the moving sidewalk,
> sitting in a chair, reading the paper, pity,
> turning a leaf to the light, arranging a thorn.   (L 33)

Stern's goal, like that of tragedy, is to "convert / death and sadness into beautiful singing" (PP 42). "There is a point," he writes, "where even Yiddish / becomes a tragic tongue" (*PP* 78). Suffering opens into catharsis, spiritual enlargement, and the encounter with transcendence.

The Stern speaker is at once a comedian and a hero: a clumsy uncle full of pranks and hocus pocus whose glasses are always falling off and a figure of mythic dimensions who, like an old god, changes form at will. In all his guises, he is a "man of the heart":

> all alone in the darkness, a man of the heart
> making plans to the end, a screen for the terror,
> a dish for the blood, a little love for strangers,
> a little kindness for insects, a little pity for the dead.   (*PP* 63)

➔II←

His Own Wild Voyage

We look before and after
   And pine for what is not;
Our sincerest laughter
   With some pain is fraught;
Our sweetest songs are those that tell
   Of saddest thoughts.
                              —Shelley, "To a Skylark"

Nostalgia once had the status of a real disease; it was diagnosed two hundred years ago as an ailment that "leaves its victims solitary, musing, and full of sighs and moans. . . ." During the Civil War, five thousand cases had to be hospitalized; fifty-eight died (Broyard 11). Today's popular culture has tamed the ailment by overexposure to old clothes and old songs. Record stores now have a section called "nostalgia"; it contains the old records we think are camp or silly. Those we still take seriously go in other categories such as jazz or rock. The emotion lost credit partly because it became difficult to separate the feeling itself from phrases such as *pine for*. The poet compelled to express nostalgia often feels he must sneak it in under the guise of irony, or through a persona, or in a web of diverting strategy.

Our distaste for nostalgia is a remnant of modernism, but the "make it new" dictum fixed on recent progenitors; it was not a denial of pastness but of continuity. The modern artist hoped to leap back across centuries, claiming an ancient and valid past. We tend to see this impulse as a continuation of the romantic embrace of primitivity. But rejection of the immediate past in favor of more distant ancestry is a feature of every period: the Renaissance rejected the medieval in favor of the classical, and the classical age itself enjoyed an imagined recollection of the golden age. The backwards quest leads ultimately to Edenic preconsciousness, that is, to paradise.

Longing to recover the lost past is inevitable in the life and art of any age, no matter how it is denied. And artists cannot escape inherited forms, which are always nostalgic; even the severe rejection of a form is a reminder of it. Writers in particular are past-bound: as Seamus Heaney notes, language is "time-charged"; it draws us into the "backward and abysm" of history (38). Jeffrey M. Perl, in *The Tradition of the Return*, treats *nostos* as a containing framework for all literature, from Homer to Joyce.

Gerald Stern has made a more extreme assertion: "Maybe the subject of the poem is always nostalgia." He decides that "conventional nostalgia fits" are echoes of the real thing, "soothing little alarums" that help us fend off serious feelings. In contrast, authentic nostalgia is "the essential memory." Its vibrance rests on a synergy of opposed yet simultaneous emotions: the pain of separation and the sweetness of remembered—or imagined—union ("Notes" 12.5: 36). His assertion is made viable when we consider nostalgia as a recognition of the paradox of consciousness. In this framework, poetry is the consequence of the Fall and always seeks to reverse it. Thus, poetry wants, ultimately, to deny itself—or exceed itself in a transforming retrieval.

Stern's emphasis on nostalgia is shared by Bachelard, who, in *The Poetics of Reverie*, places the emotion in a Jungian atmosphere. He calls it "smiling regret"; in popular talk we call it "bittersweet." This "strange synthesis of loss and consolation" is central for Bachelard because it provides access to the pure, dateless memory of a "total season" that is not "of history" but "of the cosmos." It lets us "pardon a very ancient grief" (116, 119).

For Stern, nostalgia has "great psychic roots with true and terrifying aspects of rupture and separation." We are "not just 'remembering' animals but nostalgic animals"; nostalgia is "endemic to the soul":

> I see it as an intense desire to be reunited with something in the
> universe from which we feel cut off. I see it as a search for the
> permanent. As a celebration of lost values. As a reaction to war,
> and crisis. As a reaction to disenchantment. As an escape from
> faceless society. As a reaching out for life. As a hatred of es-
> trangement. As a quest for that "other place." As a response to
> non-recognition. As a response to bourgeois indifference and
> lying, to totalitarianism, to complexity. As a dream of justice
> and happiness. As a product of slavery, of the orphanage, and
> the jail. As a smell from another world. As a combination of
> absence and presence, the far and the near, the lost and the
> found. ("Notes" 12.5: 36)

In Stern's view, nostalgia is not unprogressive. It doesn't prevent
change. It has been appropriated by rightists who put it to
"monstrous" uses, but it does not, in itself, have a moral or political
dimension. Nor is it necessarily effete; it can be empowering or irre-
solute, depending on its form and the purposes it serves ("Notes"
12.5: 36). He makes a similar distinction between trivial and strong
nostalgia in the art work. Art that presents "unconverted, unren-
dered, nostalgia" is weaker than art with a nostalgic subtext under
the apparent subject. The best poets, Stern says, are able to make
"those terrifying links between their personal loss and the great
public loss" which is exaggerated in America by "the absence of a
past" (" Notes" 12.5: 37; 12.1: 21).

In his own poems, Stern is drawn back endlessly into memory.
For him, a crucial aspect of the poet's role is to rescue and reimagine
the past: "going over the past a little, / changing a thing or two, /
making a few connections, / doing it all with balance . . ." (PP 23).
His nostalgia is distanced and tempered by the extravagant antics of
his speaker.

The speaker frets about his addiction to memory in "I Need Help
from the Philosophers" (LL 9–10). "I am still attacked by memory,"
he complains, "I am losing Blake and his action." He need only close
his eyes "for one second" to be overwhelmed by images from the
past: "I see Bobby / Wiseman stuttering through his father's old
jokes; / I see Olive Oyl sobbing behind a fence in Brutus' thick
arms. . . ." He denounces nostalgia: "I don't want to grab Dante by
the finger and ask him about my lost woods." He determines to fo-
cus on the visible: he will lie on the beach "one more time" to

"encounter the jellyfish and the fleas," to "lie in the middle of the egg capsules and the lettuce." But his attention is drawn away from these emblems of life and birth to signals of death, to "the skeletons," seashells that are reminders of the past and of death. He notices especially "the crab's thin shell."

The poem ends in longing undercut by metaphor and irony, a blend found in a number of Stern poems. The last few lines read easily, but they are a syntactical impasse:

> With all my heart I study the crab's thin shell—
> like a prostrate rabbi studying his own small markings—
> so I can rise for one good hour like him
> into a second existence, old and unchanging.

The speaker is prostrate in that he's lying on the sand; the word also suggests prayerful submission. While looking at the crab, the speaker becomes a metaphorical rabbi who studies only his own "markings," his life and also his writings. The word *markings*, however, doesn't sit well on the rabbi; it fits in an anatomical description of the crab. This is one of Stern's tricky, ingathering metaphors: speaker, rabbi, and crab are blurred through word association. Whoever he is, the speaker is caught in a solipsistic gesture brought on by memory. As the poem closes, he justifies his behavior: his motive is to achieve a brief rebirth, to rise "into a second existence, old and unchanging." The syntax continues to kid us here, since we can't be sure whether "like him" refers to the rabbi or the crab. This kind of unresolved syntax is part of Stern's signature; it challenges our faith in the substantiality of language and thereby calls into question meaning itself.

The mixed tone of the poem is also typical; we can't decide whether the longing to rise, after lying prostrate on the beach, is genuine or mocking. And in any case, the whole poem is halfway tongue-in-cheek; the speaker was never completely in earnest about his distaste for memory. If he rebukes himself, it is for relishing the trivial, personal, even comic-book memories he chooses in the opening of the poem as compared to the primordial and racial memories suggested by the crab and rabbi. Yet he doesn't admire the self-centered rabbi. The attitude toward nostalgia in this poem remains mixed; it is associated with death and also with rebirth. When we palpate a Stern poem, syntactically or tonally, it becomes unstable and dubious in a way that suggests Stevens, in spite of the very different speaker and mood. Like Stevens, Stern is dynamic rather than pictorial; both present an enactment of thought, a meditation or rumination, rather than an argument.

Throughout the canon, the Stern speaker unabashedly celebrates the blessings of nostalgic recollection, when "the heart breaks in two to the words of old songs / and the memory of other small radios in other gardens" (*LL* 26). On close inspection, however, his sentimental avowals are complicated by gentle ironies, comic self-awareness, and narrative complexity. In this case, the heart which "breaks in two" is not that of the speaker but of a man who, metaphorically, lives near him:

> On my poor road a man lives like a slug;
> he rides along the soil like an old wheel,
> leaving a trail of silver,
> and makes his home in the wet grass and the flowers.
> He is finally free of all the other mysteries
> he had accepted
> and sees himself suddenly lying there warm and happy.

This neighbor of the speaker, also one *on the same path*, is, of course, Gerald Stern. The poem illustrates how narrative mirroring distances statement in the text: the speaker sees the poet as one who "sees himself." At this point, he is immersed in nature, free of the "other mysteries." In a sense, then, he is free of consciousness and its abstractions. Yet he isn't, since it is only through consciousness that he envisions its absence. Here, Stern presents the romantic quandary of consciousness, but he does so in a poem of such apparent simplicity that the reader may not notice its duplicity. This *not noticing* or setting aside of recursive patterns is, says the poem, the only way we can have such easeful moments, and they are necessary for survival.

Stern's sentimental avowals are often paradoxical: utterly sincere and dubious at the same time. Even when they seem most pure, they are contextually undermined, within the poem and by other statements in the corpus. "The Faces I Love" (*RC* 1) is a typical pattern where negative imagery precedes a moment of nostalgic sentiment. The poem has to overcome its disavowals to achieve the good moment; it does so through shifts in diction and tone and by images

41

of death and life. As the poem opens, the speaker is in the same po-
sition as the "prostrate rabbi" discussed above. He imagines he will
lie down "like a dead man," passive, unresisting, "helpless and ex-
hausted." His attacker will take him for dead: "the leopard will walk
away from me in boredom / and trot after something living, some-
thing violent / and warm. . . ." The last lines of the poem are so ap-
pealing that we set aside these negations:

> I will pull the blinds down and watch my nose and mouth
> in the blistered glass.
> I will look back in amazement at what I did
> and cry aloud for two more years, for four more years,
> just to remember the faces, just to recall the names,
> to put them back together—
> the names I can't forget, the faces I love.

We almost fail to notice that the obvious sincerity of this ending is
tempered by recognition of solipsism. The nostalgic interlude occurs
cut off from the world, with the blinds pulled down. The speaker is
absorbed in his own reflection, which is flawed by the "blistered
glass."

When the poem mentions "the names I can't forget," it points to
the importance of proper names throughout the corpus. Names ring
in the poems like alarms going off to remind us of the depth and di-
versity of culture: Emerson and Apollo, Nietzsche and Hannibal,
Ovid and O'Neill. Shelley, Carnegie, Casimir the Great, Landor,
Debs. James, Mao Tse-tung, W. C. Handy. Galileo, Swedenborg,
Adler, Adam. He loves the names themselves, he has said, and he
loves "great minds." They are "like cities"; they are "concentrations
of energy and memory" (Hillringhouse 28). Names of places appeal
to him for the same reasons. Beside personal markers like streets,
beaches, buildings, restaurants, and the towns and cities of Amer-
ica, he places distant cities and nations: Mexico, Paris, Poland, Car-
thage, Dresden, Rome, Zimbabwe, Alexandria, and his profound
city of Crete. He does not focus on American culture alone, but on
world culture, which, in imagination, he travels and claims:

> Please forgive me, my old friends!
> I am walking in the direction of the Hopi!
> I am walking in the direction of Immanuel Kant!

> I am learning to save my thoughts—like
> one of the Dravidians—so that nothing will
> be lost, nothing I tramp upon, nothing I
> chew, nothing I remember. (R 40)

His persistent recitation of names is a way of rounding up history to save and celebrate it, creating a collaboration between past and present, historic and personal. Naming is also a mode of possession. As Barthes has it, when we name we impose on the reader the "final state of matter, that which cannot be transcended" (*Pleasure of the Text* 45).

The Stern poem typically fans out from an instigating image to a chain of association and allusion that gathers the past into the present and the imagined future, collapsing time and space, uniting subject and object. Through juxtaposition of the visible and the distant, the poet deflects lineal history, replacing it with a recurring apprehension that makes time simultaneous.

A typical portrayal of recurrence and simultaneity occurs in "Later Today" (*PP* 4). As is often the case in Stern, the experience begins in a traditional recognition of nature's cycles. The word *again*, which, like *one more time*, is a favorite of Stern's, is used as a trigger. The speaker is confident that historical time will dissolve in eternal time. The fact that this release from temporality will occur "Later Today" is a little joke. Time will be opened by looking at things "for one minute" and talking about them: "we'll sit for one minute / on the side porch and stare at the bright shadows.

> We'll start talking about the wall
> and the green pool beside the copper feeder
> and how the birch could grow again
> and how the door would look with roses on it.
> We will live in the light
> as if we were still in France,
> as if the boats were there
> and we were staring into space,
> as if we were in Babylon,
> walking beside the iron giants,
> touching their black beards,
> looking at their huge eyes,
> going down to our clay houses and our tiny cafés
> on the muddy river.

The poem creates spacious confidence. We feel opened, reading it, and we tend to ignore the fact that its calm certainty is undermined in several ways. Nature's capacity for rebirth is asserted only conditionally: the birch "could grow again." The experience told in the poem has not occurred nor is it occurring; it is characteristically posited in the future tense. And the return journey is metaphorical; we'll "live in the light" only "as if we were still in France." The same stratagems are used to qualify possibilities in Stevens, as when he writes: "There *might be*, too, a change immenser than / A poet's metaphors in which being *would* / Come true, a point in the fire of music where / Dazzle yields to a clarity. . . ." (Emphasis mine.)

The simultaneity represented, however tentatively, in "Later Today" and many other Stern poems is always presented as an occurrence in the speaker's mind, never *out there*. It is a representation of mental time, but it also suggests the mythic or primitive time admired and pursued by modern writers.

When time became historical, it became a line; that is, it became space. Ricardo Quinones is among those who describe this tyranny of history over time as a product of Renaissance rationalism, which replaced Greek myth (23–39). The discovery of perspective, which makes space rational, is often linked to the concomitant rationalization of time. Richard Palmer, for instance, asserts that perspective led to the perception of time as a "linear succession of nows" that can be measured and thereby controlled (22–24). Octavio Paz places the origins of historical time much earlier; he says "the idea of a finite and irreversible time" originated in the Fall, when each moment became distinct, severed from "the eternal present of Paradise." He is among the many modern writers who romanticize— and in a sense mythologize—mythic time, which he calls primitive time; he sees the past of the primitives as "always motionless and always present." It is cyclical, "not what happened once, but what always happens" (9–15).

By the modern period, artists felt trapped in history and became infatuated with myth. Nietzsche foresees the modernist longing for mythic time in *The Birth of Tragedy*. In Greek tragedy, he says, myth makes the present moment seem "in a certain sense timeless"; ordinary experience gains "the stamp of the eternal" (138–39). It is this effect that the moderns longed to recapture and that remains the goal of *recursiō* in Stern and others. In this sense, all our nostalgias echo the buried dream of rebirth back from passing time into

mythic time, which we might also call ideal time, a dateless paradise which stands not at the ends of history but in, behind, and beyond it.

Stern's radical nostalgia brings to mind the position of the deep image poets, who also seek a return to origins, union, timelessness. Robert Bly, for instance, describes a need to restore "a connection that has been forgotten," to go beyond consciousness and touch "something else" (21). W. S. Merwin, in an early poem, hopes to recall a state of accord imagined as "a place where I was nothing in the fullness," capable of "hearing the silence forever . . ." (36–37). Such a quest must center in nature, not culture. James Wright typifies the rejection of culture shared by many such poets. In one poem, he throws a book of bad poetry behind a stone, turning instead to the insect world: a column of ants "carrying small white petals" and old grasshoppers who "have clear sounds to make" (36).

Poetry of this sort, encouraged by Eastern religion and surrealism, often proceeds by seeking to distill or abstract out a unity hidden in nature or in the core of primordial memory. It seeks the essential through a process of exclusion and concentration, by cutting back, like trimming away at a bush to uncover its form. The success of this kind of poem rests on restraint and an often deceptive simplicity, a quality not of movement but of stillness. It can achieve the quality of purity and silence we associate with James Wright's famous "A Blessing" or with William Stafford poems such as "Looking Across the River" and "A Glass Face in the Rain." The source of this centripetal poetry is shamanistic. It relies on mythic memory, which seeks to escape history. It may be called a poetry of absence, where absence is taken to imply decreation, being removed and at rest, away from transience and singleness, in a centered, timeless, mystical or quasi-mystical harmony that resolves the quandary of consciousness.

Stern shares the goal of these poets, yet his poem is of the opposite type. His style is discursive, effusive, centrifugal, and inclusive; he appears to put in whatever comes to him as he writes. His poem is a baroque performance of elaboration or accretion which accumulates meaning as more and more material is gathered on its surface. He describes his relaxed yet active gesture as "layering on of one line after another and one idea after another by a kind of controlled association, and the delight—and terror—for me is not knowing where I'm going, even if I know what I'm doing" ("A Few Words on

Form" 146). The energy and tension of this adventure stay in the poem; they are felt by the reader. It's an untamed, unruly poem, full of sub-plots, covert signals, revisions, and reversals, yet it's supple and pleasing. I am tempted to describe it with the word *montage*, but the Stern poem is syntactic, not imagistic; continual disruptions of narration make the reader acutely aware of narrative time. I am also tempted by the word *organic*, often used to describe a poem which develops out of its own impulses rather than according to metrical, logical, or narrative patterns. But this use of the term is misleading, since plants and animals don't discover their own shapes; their forms are predetermined.[1] A better word for the Stern poem is *vocal*; we feel we are in the unmediated presence of speech as opposed to the reflective distance of writing. Barthes proposes such speech as an aspect of textual pleasure; he calls it "writing aloud." It is carried by "the *grain* of the voice" and makes us hear the "materiality" and "sensuality" of the human presence (*Pleasure of the Text* 66–67).

The discursive mode employed by Stern finds its source in the epic. This kind of poem relies on social memory, on consciousness, and typically wants to enter history, not escape it. Such poetry often has goals like those of realism in fiction, in that it exposes and defines the culture. It rests on a recognition of appearances and pays tribute to the flux; therefore, it may be called the poem of presence. It can be found in the canons of poets as dissimilar as John Hollander, Robert Lowell, Edward Dorn, Robert Pinsky, John O'Hara, and James McMichael. Stern uses this poem of presence to achieve absence; the strain of this combination is one of the sources of the uncommon quality of his work. He is often read in terms of this mode, and defined thereby as a social poet. And indeed, he can fruitfully be seen through the lens of this definition. He maps the American terrain from the perspective of a city-bred Jew transplanted to small-town life. But his emphasis is different from that of the social poet; while topical and political, his poem is also placed overtly and emphatically in the history of ideas. And it is absorbed in an even wider, mystical context. He sees no disparity among these concerns: "The reader must have the real world. He must have it for survival, he must have it because it's there. . . . And the mystic's world is the same as the agitator's world. It must be" (Hillringhouse 30).

"A Hundred Years from Now" (*RC* 56–57) is an attempt to define the spirit of America and place it in an eternal context. The speaker begins by seeking an American metaphor, a "purple sage," that will have timeless significance. He looks in nature for images that will make essential connections, so poets of ancient civilizations can understand Zane Grey:

> I myself am searching for the purple sage that I can share
> for all time with the poets of Akkadia and Sumeria.
> I am starting with my river bottom, the twisted
> sycamores and the big-leaved catalpas, making
>   the connections
> that will put Zane Grey in the right channel. I am
> watching a very ancient Babylonian who looks something
> like me or Allen Ginsberg before he shaved his beard off
> pick up *The Border Legion* and *The Riders of the Trail*
> from the dust. I am explaining him the spirit
> of America behind our banality, our devotion
> to the ugly and our suicidal urges;
> how Zane Grey, once he saw the desert,
> could not stop giving his life to it,
> in spite of his dull imagination and stilted prose;
> how the eternal is also here,
> only the way to it is brutal.
> O Babylonian, I am swimming in the deep off the island
> of my own death and birth. Stay with me![2]

Social criticism is important in the poem; however, its larger goal is to place American culture in the context of human culture and finally to absorb *chronos* in mythos. When the speaker finds himself watching a Babylonian discover a text of America—as an anthropologist might find an old Babylonian tablet—it is not that time is reversed or that the speaker has traveled back; rather, historic time has entered myth. The speaker swims in "the deep," an eternal element where death and birth—that is, rebirth—occur. He entreats the Babylonian to stay with him; he yearns to preserve the ideal time achieved in the poem.

"The New Moses" (*PP* 41) is another example of Stern as mythmaker. It begins with some cattails struggling to survive near an airport, "putting up with the noise of engines." These mere weeds, representatives of nature, will survive the technological landscape:

"They will be all that's left / when the airport is dismantled / and the city is gone / and the roads are ruined and scattered." The cattails remind the speaker of the Moses story; he imagines that "some new Moses will float by" and be found by a princess who will make her way

> down through the buried brick and iron
> on the almost forgotten fringes of modern Thebes,
> not far from the man-made islands and lost skyways,
> the hundred heavily guarded tunnels and bridges,
> of ancient New York.

American civilization is doomed, like all others, in its temporal existence. But it takes its place as part of civilization itself, an idea and a story that is permanent, recurring. In his uses of history to mold an ahistorical drama, Stern is most like the Eliot of *The Waste Land*, the Eliot who said: "Only through time is time conquered." Stern's America is also like Joyce's Dublin in that it is both history and myth.

American culture is but a surface subject of Stern, albeit an extremely important one. It is a manifestation of his preoccupation with the larger melting pot of human culture which becomes synchronous in his work. His obsession is not so much the past itself as the relationship between presence and memory, history and myth, conscious and unconscious, surface and depth. This is why his brand of nostalgia naturally couches the pursuit of ideal time or absence in a social poetry of presence. He demonstrates that social memory can be assimilated in mythic memory.

This assimilation is accomplished partly by leveling, which erases patterns like chronology and hierarchy that typify social thought, dissolving them in unifying myth. The huge historical events Stern refers to are no more or less important than his walks along the street, his communion in the garden. Scale collapses, but events are not flattened; they are enlarged in an ardent scrutiny.

An eloquent example is "John's Mysteries" (*PP* 46–48), where the parking lot of John's, an Iowa City grocery, is transformed into a restaurant on Crete. Like most of Stern's poems, it opens in a mundane incident. The speaker is standing in line at the grocery, but he's lost: "I forget where it is I am." He has seen the same tombstone beef sticks and catalpa trees in so many cities that he could be anywhere—or everywhere. He asserts the poet's prerogative to impose his will on appearances: "I will insist on emptying the parking lot / of the two beer trucks and putting a table there / under the cigar tree, for me and my friends to eat at." Nostalgia in Stern isn't merely passive. It's a willed yet receptive gesture which invites transcendence but recognizes that it must be imaginatively prepared for.

The poem continues in a future tense that immediately spawns a past tense; the spirit of transformation is encapsulated in the syntax. The friends *will* become nostalgic, both happy and sad, and preserve what it *was* like. They will "write, in ink, what it was like to live here

> on Gilbert Street and Market, on Sixth and Pine,
> in a town in Crete eight miles from Omalos,
> a mile or so from the crone and her great-granddaughter
> selling warm Coca-Colas on the flat
> at the end of the deepest gorge in Europe—
> if Crete is in Europe—at a lovely table with lights
> hanging from the trees, a German there to remind us
> of the Parachute Corps in 1941,
> a Turk for horror, a Swede for humor, an Israeli
> to lecture us, the rest of us from New Jersey
> and California and Michigan and Georgia,
> eating the lamb and drinking the wine, adoring it,
> as if we were still living on that sea,
> as if in Crete there had not been a blossom,
> as if it had not fallen in Greece and Italy,
> some terrible puzzle in great Knossos
> Sir Arthur Evans is still unravelling,
> the horrors spread out in little pieces
> as if it were a lawn sale or foreclosure.

The *here* in the beginning of this section is delocalized; it is a house where Stern lived for a time on Gilbert Street in Iowa City, his carlier address at Sixth and Pine in Philadelphia, and also Crete.[3] The poem begins its wild, centrifugal motion, becoming global and international, erasing history, as if Crete had not spawned Greek culture and then the Renaissance, as if Crete had not contained the puzzle of origins which its archaeologist, Sir Arthur Evans, pieced together to create history out of silence.

The poem moves next to a meditation on Sir Arthur Evans, a representative of historic time who is imagined "putting together our future." The group of friends watch "with curiosity and terror, / wondering if he'll get it right, wondering how much / it's really in his hands, wanting a little / to tamper with it. . . ." They long to replace historic time with ideal, mythic time:

> wanting it to be as it once was,
> wanting the bull to bellow,
> wanting him to snort and shake the ground,
> wanting it to be luminous again . . .

But Sir Arthur Evans "finds another fragment / that tells him something." He becomes the "angel of death": history is death.

The poem returns to the present tense and the everyday world as the poet-speaker heads back to his home on Gilbert Street. The use of tenses as a framework for movement between ordinary and radiant experience is common in Stern. He moves from present to future tense when he moves into past events that are intense; more than a time of arrival, his is a future from which the past is validated. His *I will go back* syntax emphasizes the exercise of will in his return journey; it also asserts that the past is in the future, that time is achronous.

All this seems natural, inevitable, as it spins out in the progress of a meditation that sounds like a spontaneous overflow of talk. Sometimes tentative "asides" are included to display the speaker's fumbling attempts to get things straight. In the opening of this poem, for instance, when he's not sure which store he's in, he says, "I think it was Bishop's," shifting momentarily to past tense as if to let us know that the present tense of the poem is being invented. Sometimes the speaker stumbles and corrects himself. When he talks about the friends who watch Sir Arthur Evans "putting together" the future, he says "the seven of us." This sounds wrong to the reader, who turns back to the part where the friends are enumerated and counts eight. Stern immediately corrects himself: "the seven of us, / the eight of us, by the sea." Leaving this mistake in place attests to the poem's authenticity as a record of thought.

The speaker returns to Gilbert Street, transformed through his role as actor on the stage of the poem. Now he is "balanced forever / between two worlds," past and present, dailiness and myth, reality and imagination. He sees himself in the historical maps (charts) of Crete; he is a drop of white paint on the page which metamorphoses into images of increasing forcefulness: "I walk

> up Gilbert Street to reach my house. I live
> with music now, and dance, I lie alone
> waiting for sweetness and light. I'm balanced forever
> between two worlds, I love what we had, I love
> dreaming like this, I'm finding myself in the charts
> between the white goat and the black, between
> the trade with Sicily and the second palace, between
> the wave of the sea and the wave of the sky, I am
> a drop of white paint, I am the prow of a ship,
> I am the timbers, I am the earthquake—

The future tense resumes as he imagines that someone will eventually see *him* in a dream of Crete like the "dream" which is this poem. The celebration of remembrance will continue in cyclical time as he greets that dreamer. He, the poet, will again transform the ordinary parking lot. He will do this by touching the beer trucks with his left and right hands, a kind of ritual gesture that recurs throughout Stern. He will be ancient and venerable, a stone god who embraces the dreamer and sings (that is, does poetry) to make him remember the beef sticks and catalpa tree that opened the poem. The return of images from the early lines closes the associative cycle of the poem; it also suggests, mysteriously, that the dreamer he greets in the future-past is himself. Another "wild voyage" into ideal time—another poem—is over.

> in eighty or ninety years
> someone will dream of Crete again and see me
> sitting under this tree and study me
> along with the baskets and the red vases.
> I'll walk across here touching one beer truck
> with my left hand and one with my other.
> I'll put my old stone arms around his neck
> and kiss him on the lip and cheek, I'll sing
> again and again
> until he remembers me, until he remembers
> the green catalpa pushing through the cement
> and the little sticks of meat inside, his own
> wild voyage behind him, his own sad life ahead.

This performance is complete, but we are meant to see it as a temporal manifestation of an archetype that is always potential: everything happens again, everywhere, is happening now, will happen, always happens.

The backwards quest of "John's Mysteries" is emotional archaeology, set against the historic archaeology of Sir Arthur Evans, which the poem mistrusts. The radiant experience unearthed in the poem is of a kind sought by so many twentieth-century writers that it must be called definitive. It's a release from estrangement that elicits and contains the quality of belief without assigning it an object. Among the many names given it by writers and critics, the most convenient, in spite of its overuse, is still epiphany. In his book-length discussion of the subject, Morris Beja stresses examples that include recapture or recreation of the past along with "the notion of the psychological coexistence of all time" (15, 27). An epiphany of this kind is, of course, inherently nostalgic.

The connection between nostalgia and epiphany is an underlying current throughout Stern, but only in *Paradise Poems* does he engage in lengthy, detailed portrayals of transfiguration. A central example is "Three Skies" (*PP* 74–76). Here, he calls his timeless moment "my lightness," a phrase that combines illumination with the sensation of near weightlessness. As in "John's Mysteries," Crete is the alembic source. The speaker seeks to understand its importance in the second long section of the poem:

> In Crete the heart gets filled up, there is a joy
> there, it is the mountains and sea combined,
> it is the knowledge you have that there was a life
> there for centuries, half unknown to Europe, half
> unknown to Asia, Crete is a kind of moon
> to me, a kind of tiny planet,
> going through the same revolutions, over and over.

Stern's fascination for Greece is similar in some ways to that of Keats in "Ode on a Grecian Urn," which, as Seamus Heaney notes, does not stem from a sense of "belonging to a particular place" or from "the burden of a particular history":

> Historical Greece may have provided images for his daydream
> but transfigured Greece, under the aspect of the urn, awakened
> his imaginative and intellectual appetites. . . . Keats' past is
> closer to the long-ago of fairy-tale and functions in his mind as
> a source of possibility, a launch pad for transcendence. (38)

Like Keats, Stern loves Greece because it helps him achieve "lightness." But Stern's poem is far more personal and idiosyncratic than its romantic precursor. It rests on close details of his visits to Greece rather than on the import of a cultural symbol like the Elgin marbles. Yet it is not about Stern's private life; it is a dramatization of consciousness.

The pattern of "Three Skies" is the same as that of "John's Mysteries," but in this case the speaker describes the epiphany besides enacting it. Both poems begin in a place where food is sold; this site, usually a restaurant, is a favorite of the poet's. Here, it's Dante's, a Greenwich Village coffee house. The tense is the same continual present that appears in "John's Mysteries" and throughout the canon: "I always remember," "I always think," "I sit." While he sits there in Dante's, his "left hand is walking through Crete" and his "right hand is lying exhausted on the roof / looking up at the stars." The word *stars* triggers a memory of the first time he had his lightness in Greece. He shifts to the past tense:

> It was the stars
> that helped me then. I stood on the cracked cement
> on the same hill I know where Minos stood
> looking for heavenly bulls and for the first time
> in Greece I had my lightness. I saw the link
> between that life and mine. I saw the one
> outside me stand for my own, like Dante himself
> in Paradise. I felt I was standing inside
> the sky, that there were other lights below me
> and other worlds and this one could be restored.
> And there were other feelings I have forgotten
> or can't quite put in words. I saw myself
> moving from body to body. I saw my own
> existence taken from me. I lost the center.

This supranatural integration approaches literal transcendence when the speaker imagines himself up in the sky. This kind of "upwards fall" has been described by a number of critics; it contrasts with the downward fall into time and knowledge. Paul de Man says that poetic transcendence is like a "spontaneous ascent" and resembles an "act of grace" (46). Stern's out-of-body experience might seem silly or pretentious were it not for the conversational earnestness with which he confides what he "can't quite put in words."

The speaker recalls that the uplifting accord "lasted for fifteen minutes." Then he slept on the roof—seemingly the same roof where his right hand lay open at the start of the poem—though at that point he was sitting in a coffee shop. This knocks out the distinction between the present time of the poem and the time of the remembered "lightness." He remembers "going into lying still, / going into some secret humming and adoring, / I was so changed, I was so small and silent." This typical Sternian reference to esoteric, prayerful ritual is a response to *being changed* in the course of the poem.

A few lines later, as the third and last section opens, the poem shifts back to Dante's Café. But it does not shift back to the present tense; the new section is continuous with the Crete narrative. This seems to undermine the distinctness and validity of the transcendent event.

> It wasn't lost on me that it was Dante's
> Café that I was sitting in—a coffee house
> in Greenwich Village with an overblown photo
> of Florence on the wall, squeezed in among
> my loved ones, reading books, or talking, or waiting
> for someone to come, for someone new to walk in
> and catch our interest, the irony—even the comedy—
> wasn't lost on me. I think I had been there
> over an hour frowning and writing. It was
> a disgrace! Thank God for New York! Thank God for tolerance!

These lines remind us that the ecstatic incident occurred, as far as the narrative field of the poem goes, in the everyday world of books and talk at Dante's. They remind us that, in fact, the incident is purely verbal, a poem written in a café: "I think I had been there for over an hour, thinking and writing." The self-deflating, amused tone of the lines further weakens the epiphany. The speaker wants us to know that he understands the irony and comedy of his situation.

After a characteristic link back to motifs introduced in the opening, the poem gears up into a typical Stern resolution, one of his most beautiful:

I walk
through the cement playground at Sixth and Houston and down
to Vandam Street. My poem is over. My life
is on an even keel, though who's to say
when I will waver again. I start to call
my friends up one at a time to talk about the stars,
my friends on the Upper West Side and my friends in
    the Village,
my friends in New Jersey and Brooklyn. I listen
    to them rave,
those poor stargazers, everyone with a story,
everyone either a mystic or a poet,
one a musician, one an astrologer,
all of them illuminated, all of them ecstatic,
every one changed, for a minute, by his own memory.

The interlude of paradisical harmony enacted so fully in the above poems is often suggested more briefly. The Stern corpus, like those of Stevens and Joyce, is a web of cross-references where an element that appears quickly, sometimes mysteriously, in one place may be fully explicated in another. The canon constantly clarifies, reinforces, and comments on itself; this criss-crossing movement tends to make the whole body of work synchronic.

For instance, detailed familiarity with Stern's epiphany enhances our response to a poem like "Magritte Dancing" (*RC* 26–27). The passing reference to Crete in this poem is enriched by what we learn about its significance in "John's Mysteries," which was written later. "Magritte Dancing" presents a more humble and low-key version of transcendence than the poems we've looked at. It illustrates how the artist, through the expansive movement of his mind, can escape everyday life. It starts as the speaker goes to bed tired and angry and is annoyed when his wife turns the light on and trips over his shoes. Unable to sleep, he watches the dark until dawn. His mind moves gradually away from the present and toward nature: "I am thinking again about snow tires, and I am thinking / about downtown Pittsburgh and I am thinking / about the turtles swimming inside their brown willows." He begins an imaginative dance "to the tune of Magritte," that is, to the tune of art. He imagines Oskar Schlemmer and Pablo Picasso; these proper names come in typically to expand the poem through the speaker's realization of his continuity with others. He moves from the constrictions of private life into the shared life of history and culture, finally becoming timeless and global as he enacts Edenic clarity and perfection:

> I dance on the road and on the river and
> in the wet garden, all the time living in Crete
> and pre-war Poland and outer Zimbabwe,
> as through my fingers and my sparkling hair
> the morning passes, first the three loud calls
> of the bluejay, then the white door slamming,
> then the voices rising and falling in sudden harmony.

Here the *recursiō*, a gesture both willed and fortuitous, opens into a radiant apprehension of paradise.

In Stern's plot, we are lucky to have lost paradise. It is a nostalgic entity which exists because it is lost. We are lucky to suffer, since suffering is what we transcend. Acknowledgment and acceptance of suffering is our humanity, our victory. This is a version of the romantic vision, and it is also the tragic vision, in which spiritual redemption is won through noble suffering.

It is also a traditional vision, a poetic program so overworked that it seems too old hat to survive without irony or other procedures of extreme deflation. Stern's enactment of it is tinged with a chuckle of self-parody, yet it remains serious. His tactic is to go the other way, to crank up such an orchidaceous display of nostalgic sentiment that we are asked to admire his daring. He uses the word *sweet*, for instance, again and again, hoping we'll forgive it of his lovable, clumsy, yet obviously erudite speaker.

His success depends on the originality and authenticity of this voice; it produces a surrealism of wit, a zany flux of rhetoric that beguiles us in spite of ourselves.[4] This speaker, like other victims of nostalgia, is "solitary, musing, full of sighs and moans" (Broyard 11). He's also an exhibitionist, loquacious and playful, whimsical and wise. Extravagance is often associated, nowadays, with insincerity, but Stern's flamboyance is not feigned, nor is his belief in the mediating force of nostalgic memory, "always seeing the heart / and what it wanted, the beautiful, cramped heart."

➔III←

The Man with the Rake

The garden is one of our most tempting messages, one of the signals which underlies all our elaborations. A space, an idea, and a story, it encourages several impulses toward speech: the need to describe or penetrate, the wish to consider, and the urge to narrate or carry forward. A vessel for our great stories of perfection and betrayal, ruin and transformation, flesh and spirit, origins and destiny, the ordinary garden and the garden of origins to which it refers unite passing time and timelessness, seasonal recurrence and seasonless perfection. Behind the pictorial, philosophical, and narrative sources of garden imagery are even older reverberations of incantation: planting and harvest rituals wherein poetry and worship are joined.

Yet the garden is dangerous territory for the poet. Because it is such an ancient, rich, familiar, and beloved symbol, our response to it is conventionalized. To recover its innocence, our typified response has to be interrupted. This is one of the responsibilities of the poet in Western culture and in modern times: to redeem the innate, irrevocable symbols without which we are forlorn.

Because his imagination is compelled by community, celebration, and vision, Stern is drawn to fundamental symbols. The garden, in particular, is for him an inevitable figure: here his tragi-comic hero enacts the *chorismos*, the drama of the consequences of separation from god, from spirit. For Stern, the condition of exile is "in the very nature of the human" ("Notes" 12.5: 36). The nostalgic impulse at the center of his work springs from a buried memory or dream of earliness and permanence. The spiritual transformation he seeks is a return to the essence of that memory, the timeless perfection and union envisioned as an "amorous summer" without which we are transient and unanchored, like squirrels who "live from roof to roof":

> We sigh for some understanding, some surcease,
> some permanence, as we move from tree to tree,
> from wire to wire, from empty hole to empty hole,
> singing, singing, always singing, of that amorous summer. (*RC* 10)

Other concerns important to Stern emerge from this center: the theme of the artist-creator, immersion in recurring nature, the issue of pastoral in the urban landscape, the Jew as exile. His garden is an actual patch of ground, a symbol of recurrence and union, and a metaphor for the poem itself. His poem sometimes becomes a corner of paradise:

> This is a corner of heaven here,
> the moss growing under the leaves,
> the rocks cropping up like small graves under the trees,
> the old giants rotting in the shade. (*R* 70)

"Old giants" appear in at least one other poem (*LL* 21), where they are black locust trees. In Stern's private symbolism, this is the Jewish tree. They are also old heroic figures or gods.

Stern's poem becomes the world—not this world but a transformed version of it. He doesn't have a contained, real place that becomes his mythic territory, as does the Dublin of Joyce, the New England of Frost, or the Mexico of Carlos Fuentes. There is a sense in which the whole American terrain is his figurative landscape; here he shares the traditional vision of the American continent as a paradise regained and subsequently lost. Yet he places this landscape in wider contexts that are global and historic. What he does is to overlay all his settings with a mythic topography at the crux of which is the *topos* of the garden. In a denial of the alienation so definitive of modern experience, he is obviously at home in his invented realm.

The Man with the Rake

Stern's response to the garden is rarely pictorial or familiar. He designifies and revitalizes it in various ways: by introducing surprise elements, impeding the course of the poem through digressive interruption of statement and action, condensing some parts while elaborating others, suppressing certain references so that only a hint or shadow is disclosed, complicating time and space through use of simultaneous action, interfering with expectations about language and tone. These familiar devices rarely strike us as agonistic in Stern; they seem inevitable gestures of the speaker. The speaker goes beyond description and narration to enact—to live through—his garden adventure.

Stern comments on the distinction between drained romantic imagery and his own lived imagery in "Planting Strawberries" (*R* 57):

> If this is a thing of the past,
> planting strawberries on the Delaware River
> and eating zucchini from my own garden,
> then I will have to be buried too,
> along with the beer-hall musicians
> and the "startlingly beautiful sunset"

The poet would rather be buried under accusations of defunct romanticism than to relinquish his "own garden"—the life and work he has chosen.

In some poems, the Stern speaker observes the garden with meditative intensity: "For hours I sit here facing the white wall / and the dirty swallows. If I move too much, / I will lose everything . . ." (*PP* 28). He sometimes imagines he "could live like that, / putting my chair by the window, / making my tea, / letting the light in, / trapping the spider in my left hand" (*PP* 37). In a deprived season, when the garden is dead, he can subsist on mental nourishment alone; his mind can invent a garden:

> I live in the brain,
> drinking its water,
> eating its rich food,
> waiting for it to send out its small pulses
> and find good furrows for the threads to root in,
> waiting for it to search through the wet patches
> and bring back fresh mud, and flowers, to my bed. (*LL* 17)

59

The passive, receptive imagination appears often in Stern; the speaker lies in bed or sits in his chair so often that it seems a definitive posture. In an essay, Stern even calls himself a "recumbent angel" ("Notes" 13.1: 17). But in fact, this posture provides weight in a corpus of continual movement, both syntactic and dramatic. The speaker's passive imagination is overshadowed by a willful and potent one. In his strongest enactments, the two are joined in a stance both receptive and willful.

The most powerful role taken by Stern's garden speaker is that of the godly artist-creator. The title poem of *Rejoicings* (R 11–12) is a gently parodic, half-comic reenactment of creation itself, overlaid on a scene at the beach where Stern used to vacation. The poet-god arranges the world in a painterly composition: "I put the sun behind the Marlborough Blenheim / so I can see the walkers settling down / to their long evening of relaxation / over the slimy piers."[1] He goes on to "put the clouds in their place and start the ocean / on its daily journey. . . ."

Having made a world, he places an Adam in it. He uses a "broken stick," a primitive form of his usual pencil, to draw a circle in the sand: "so I can close the whole world in my grip / and draw my poor crumbling man / so that his tears fall within the line." This line suggests the circumference of the circle in which Renaissance artists placed the male figure.[2] It also refers to the poetry line, in which the poet creates a man in his image: "my poor crumbling man" suggests the speaker himself.

His work is blurred by feeling. His medium, the sand, is "half out of focus"; it "lightens and darkens" with emotion, "the clouds and the sun." His art fills him with the tragic emotions: it "takes all I have of pity and fear." There are storm clouds, "a few black puffs, the end of some great violence," that "blow into the wind before their dispersal."[3] Filled with the "craziness" of emotion injected into art, the speaker is led to gestures of belief. He pantomimes a prayer: "I move my lips and raise my quiet hand." He has "come back one more time to the shore . . . like a believer—to squeeze the last poetry out of the rubbish." The faith which once inspired art has become mere rubbish, the artist a tragi-comic player who goes through the motions of belief.

Having created an American Adam, he decides to offer him salvation through a decent burial in the sand. The first step is a cleansing ritual: "I pour a little mud on my head / for the purification /

and rub the dirty sand into my shirt / to mix everything with crystal." The speaker prepares the body for life after death:

> I put a piece of shell for killing birds
> in the open hand
> and all the paraphernalia of the just,
> bottle and paper and pencil,
>
> for the work to come.
> I wait one hour. That is the time it takes
> to free the soul, the time it takes
> for reverence.

Among the necessaries for rebirth are the paper and pencil of the poet.

In the penultimate line, the speaker suddenly realizes it is "our Nietzsche" he is burying. Stern often pays tribute to Nietzsche, especially in the earlier work. Anti-determinist ideas enacted in the corpus, such as the concept of eternal recurrence and the preference for instinct, will, and action over logical causality, stem from Nietzsche as well as from older sources. "Rejoicings" is in part a drama of these ideas. "Nietzsche" is also a private reference to Stern's friend Bob Summers, who committed suicide in Philadelphia in 1972.[4]

The poem is a half-playful escalation of playing in the sand to acts of magnitude. Eternal recurrence appears as a self-begetting gesture; man reenacts the myth of creation, death, and rebirth as he makes and destroys himself, an image drawn and rubbed out in the sand. This image is also an art object, illogical and instinctive, made playfully. It represents the nexus between playfulness and artistic creation that is crucial throughout Stern and significant in art of the twentieth century. As Michel Benamou points out, play is "a Nietzschean affirmation occupying the void left by the death of god" which helps us to "extricate ourselves from strict positivistic causality . . ." (4). The ludenic aspect of art is displayed more subtly in later Stern, as the speaker becomes more sure of himself in his embodiment of the playful, yet deeply serious poet. His playfulness serves to designify his performance, but it is also an aesthetic statement.

Stern never again permits his speaker to play god in an extended scene like that of the early "Rejoicings." But intimations of godhood appear here and there in the poems, mixed with other themes. In "The Rose Warehouse" (*RC* 66–67), the speaker wants to put "my own head, / the head of Gerald Stern" on the side of a warehouse: "I want to see if he's a god / and feels like murmuring a little in the lost tongue. . . ." In "82/83" (*PP* 54–55), mouth-to-mouth resuscitation recalls God's passage of life to Adam. The speaker wants to look for a "frightened animal" and give it life, but "it's too late to breathe / into his bony mouth." In "Two Trees" (*PP* 68), a poem of dawn and spring filled with paradisical imagery, the speaker briefly resembles a god in manly form: "I walk / like a man, like a human being, through the curled flowers. . . ."

"The Expulsion" (*PP* 81–83) is an Edenic lament of the dispossessed in which the speaker begins as a godlike artist-creator but evolves into Adam. A number of Stern poems are evoked by music and painting; this one is inspired by Masaccio's *The Expulsion from Paradise*, c. 1427, a fresco in the Brancacci Chapel of the Sta. Maria del Carmine, in Florence. Stern visited the chapel in 1950, at age twenty-five, and again in 1954.

The speaker begins by emphasizing the struggle involved in his nostalgic enterprise:

> I'm working like a dog here, testing my memory,
> my mouth is slightly open, my eyes are closed,
> my hand is lying under the satin pillow.
> My subject is loss, the painter is Masaccio,
> the church is the Church of the Carmine, the narrow panel
> is on the southwest wall, I make a mouth
> like Adam, I make a mouth like Eve, I make
> a sword like the angel's. Or Schubert; I hear him howling
> too, there is a touch of the Orient
> throughout the great C major. I'm thinking again
> of poor Jim Wright and the sheet of tissue paper
> he sent me. Lament, lament, for the underlayer
> of wallpaper, circa 1935.
> Lament for the Cretans, how did they disappear?
> Lament for Hannibal. . . .

This opening places the source of nostalgic quest in the story of the expulsion and demonstrates the central Sternian method, a discursive mental-verbal movement that is both willed and receptive. It's like shining a spotlight on all the associations that pop up, until something important happens. In this case, the idiosyncratic chain of associations exposed on the poem's surface—Masaccio, the church in Italy, Eden, Schubert, Jim Wright, wallpaper, the Cretans, Hannibal—leads inward from the shared, mythic loss of paradise to an examination of private loss.

The poem is also about itself, about making the art object that is the poem. When, in the opening, the speaker makes a mouth *like* Adam and one *like* Eve, he stresses the imitative aspect of art as well as the godlike creativity of the artist-maker. Further on, he again stresses his power when he says: "*my hand* is drawing in the eyes, *I'm making* the stripes." (My emphasis.) He is appropriating the painting as he writes the poem. He admits also that his art is emotional; it moves him to tears: "I'm lying alone with water falling down / the left side of my face."

He goes on to express his love for the painting and his compassion for Adam and Eve as depicted in it: "the grief / of her slanted eyes" and "poor Adam's face / half buried in his hands. . . ." These are accurate descriptions of the figures in the painting, but his impression of the angel is distorted. In the Masaccio, she is a gentle, hovering figure, in spite of her sword and her pointing finger; in the poem she is "an angry mother" with a cruel face, who may stem from Stern's childhood memories.

The speaker becomes the Adam of the painting, and the Edenic drama merges with Stern's family drama: "my father / and I are leaving Paradise, an angel / is shouting, my hand is on my mouth. . . ." The speaker laments his lost sister, his lost father, who "had / fifty-eight suits, and a bronze coffin," and the lost paradise of childhood.

The angel provides a brief, epiphanic transport in which the poet-speaker is reunited with his father:

> Our lives are merging, our shoes
> are not that different. The angel is rushing by,
> her lips are curled, there is a coldness, even
> a madness to her, Adam and Eve are roaring,
> the whole thing takes a minute, a few seconds,
> and we are left on somebody's doorstep . . .

The angel becomes a figure for art, or imagination, which instigates a synthesis in which father and son enjoy a nostalgic reunion. They return to the "narrow garden" of an "old row house," which "no one has modernized." The chain of remembrance continues as the father remembers his own childhood home with its "giant garden." The past recovered and reconciled in the conjunction of nostalgia and art enters the Edenic myth:

> It is
> a paradise, I'm sure of it. I kiss
> him goodbye, I hold him, almost like the kiss
> in 1969, in Philadelphia,
> the last time I saw him . . .

The overt, sustained encounter with private history seen in this poem is unusual for Stern. It is not intended to singularize his life, but to mythicize it, to establish communion with all lives, all our loss. The poem ends in a recognition of others: "the families weeping beside us, the way they do, / the children waving goodbye, the lovers smiling, / the way they do, all our loss, everything / we know of loneliness."

"The Expulsion" is a dramatization of Adam's recovery of the lost garden; as such, it is a model for Stern's motive in art. It exemplifies the pause in which we regain assent to what we are part of, as we move through what Stern calls, in the final lines, "the secret rooms, the long and brutal corridor / down which we sometimes shuffle and sometimes run."

Neither godhood nor the Adamic figure is an appropriate role for the Stern speaker as he evolves in the corpus. Godhood is too stately, Adam too boring and innocuous. A more suitable garden figure is that of the gardener himself, a neighborly, backyard guy who is yet the initiator and authority figure whose power and judgment control events:

> I am the man with the rake, bent over with
> emotional neck pains, standing in my yard getting
> ready to be a garden adviser and a river prophet. (RC 50)

This declaration begins with a bold assertion of being and masculine will but is quickly softened by "getting ready," a reminder of the preparation required of a guide.

The difference between the perspective of Stern's gardener and the more usual, untrained observer of the garden is emphatic. The gardener represents a synthesis like that in *Huckleberry Finn* between the point of view of the riverboat passenger and its pilot: the passenger view is romantic, idealized, not operative, but the pilot's observations have to do with dangerous shoals and currents. The passenger's view is too picturesque and sentimental, the pilot's too matter-of-fact. These views depict two relations with nature: the elite and proprietary appreciation of the surface, the respectful and probing awareness of depth.[5] Stern, like Clemens, synthesizes the two in a first-person speaker whose voice is unusual and authentic, whose experience is lyrical but is also a matter of survival.

"For Night to Come" (*RC* 84–85) is an important illustration of the garden lesson in Stern, which always evolves into spiritual instruction. We tend to accept its fabular dimension because of its expertise as down-to-earth garden direction:

> I am giving instructions to my monkey
> on how to plant a pine tree. I am telling
> him to water the ground for hours before
> he starts to dig and I am showing him
> how to twist the roots so the limbs will bend
> in the right direction.

This opening could be straight from a garden manual were it not for the fact that you don't teach a monkey how to plant a tree. Alberta Turner suggests that "the monkey and the *I* are one and the same. The monkey is the speaker's more vulnerable and primitive part" (*45 Contemporary Poems* 214). In her view, the monkey is "only himself"; the speaker is alone, signifying "that we're alone in the universe" ("Poetry 1981" 73). But the poem couldn't be about alienation; it bulges with contact, as the man and his monkey share sentimental memories, make a "nest in a clearing," lie on their backs, hold hands, tremble, feel lost, love each other, and finally look forward to a ceremonial planting that will join them in spiritual renewal. All this has the feel of a love poem intensified by dissimulation.

Stern has said the poem records a literal experience: "It was a real being I was with there, not a figment or a fragment or an idea." The incident was an actual scene of instruction: "I was teaching my monkey how to plant a pine tree; . . . we *were* stealing a tree, . . . so I could plant it in my back yard." The lesson is "technical," he says, but also about "life and death and love and survival" (*45 Contemporary Poems* 215–16). There is always a factual level in the Stern poem; even when unrecognizable, the *sens propre* plays against the *sens figuré*, adding firmness.

The actual event of "For Night to Come" took place in the Pine Barrens, a huge forest in southern New Jersey that is for Stern a central symbolic territory.[6] It stands for the presence of the wilderness in the civilized world, for the unconscious, "the primitive, the other." He and the monkey "went through a descent together" and emerged "true equals," though he "was once the teacher, the father" (215, 217).

The monkey was inspired by a Chinese drawing Stern saw years before in the Metropolitan Museum; he recalls the title as "Poet Giving Instructions to his Monkey." It suggests to Stern a whole body of material, from the monkey mythology of Africa and Asia to "the organ grinder's little assistant, with his hat and his tin cup," to "the Lou Lehr special on Saturday afternoon: 'Monkies iz the cwaziest people.'" Stern doesn't identify his real companion, but he (she?) is "my soul": "tender and loving and helpless, an utterly trusting and believing 'student'" (215–16).

The poem's success rests on the figurative potential of the unexpected monkey, with its suggestions of a playful, mischievous child; its fabular intimations; its hint of a good, prehuman past. The real "monkey" and the actual adventure also throw signals onto the surface, as does the buried information about the forest setting and the Chinese painting. This heavy, multilayered substratum, typical in Stern, complicates our response even when it is not evident.

The ending of "For Night to Come" illustrates another of Stern's standard procedures: enactment of ritual to enlarge meaning:

> and only when we have made the first cut
> and done the dance
> and poured in the two bushels of humus
> and the four buckets of water
> and mixed it in with dirt and tramped it all down
> and arranged and rearranged the branches
> will we lie back and listen to the chimes
> and stop our shaking

and close our eyes a little
and wait for night to come
so we can watch the stars together,
like the good souls we are,
a hairy man and a beast
hugging each other in the white grass.

The little reversal that makes the man hairy rather than the beast exemplifies the small surprises that occur throughout Stern, almost unnoticed, yet valuable as designifiers. The loving relationship between pupil and guide is confirmed and elevated through active work, labor that is sanctified by ritual.

It is through participation, not observation, that Stern's gardener joins most fully in nature. In "Bee Balm" (*PP* 33), for instance, he begins by "sticking a shovel in the ground" to dig up "the little green patch / between the hosta and the fringe bleeding heart." He will "plant bee balm there / and a few little pansies till the roots take / and the leaves spread out in both directions."

Here, as in "For Night to Come," his confidence as maker and prophet of the garden is authenticated by his knowledge of plants. The literal opening has worth purely as enactment of the actual garden. But it also provides strong support for the typical, outward movement of the poem, as the speaker explains the reasons for his actions: "This is so the hummingbird will rage / outside my fireplace window . . . so I can reach my own face up to his / and let him drink the sugar from my lips." Bee balm is an aromatic plant that attracts bees and hummingbirds; planting it will bring the hummingbird to his lips. That is, active participation, as opposed to passive reflection, leads to a sensual connection with the natural world.

Sensual involvement leads to a further movement into spirit:

This is so I can lie down on the couch
beside the sea horse and the glass elephant,
so I can touch the cold wall above me
and let the yellow light go through me,
so I can last the rest of the summer on thought,
so I can live by secrecy and sorrow.

The active participant earns the right to passive reflection; he can "lie down on the couch" and find enlightenment. As the light passes through him, he survives the summer, his life, in thought. In its arc from the overt to the secret, from physical action to sensual involvement to spiritual and philosophical meditation, the poem displays Stern's emphasis on the interdependence of our concrete, bodily selves and the unseen, secret selves of thought and spirit.

Crucial in Stern's union with nature is the traditional celebration of seasonal recurrence as a way to resolve the opposed garden lessons of birth and death, sweetness and sorrow. In "One More Time the Lambs" (RC 21), everything is happening again:

> One more time the hard green daffodils are growing
> in clumps beside the stone wall and the cesspool.
> They go with the melancholy and the cold rain,
> with the black trees and the frozen seedpods.

"One more time" is a persistent phrase in Stern, both a recognition and a plea. Here the sweet daffodils "go with" the sorrowful winter; recurrence unites life and death. Repetition is reinforced in the poem by repeated use of the word *again*, as the speaker determines to "go through it with ease, / no bitterness and no indecision this time." "It" is the seasonal passage and also the poem. As usual, the speaker is helped through it by the incorporation of ritual; the ancient sacrifice of the lamb occurs in preparation for another spring:

> One more time the lamb rests his soft head
> on the stone culvert, one more time he lies there
> cool and thoughtful, one more time he drops his red blood
> on the dirty ice. . . .

Rituals are recurring, metaphorical gestures, theatrical repetitions that dramatize recurring events in nature and in faith. They are solacing reminders of origins; they resolve contradiction; they legitimatize our habitation. Potent and magical, they can make things actually happen. They are staged events that can be far more real, far more significant and overwhelming, than ordinary reality. To participate in some rituals is to commit your life—even to risk your life.

In one sense, the typical Stern poem not only incorporates ritual but is itself a ritual. "One More Time the Lambs" can be seen as the kind of ritual performance that involves genuine risk and commitment. It ends in affirmation: "The wind is my love, / the rain is my love, the torn lamb is my love. . . . I wake up singing, floating, bursting, inside my sweet shelter."

Stern is not altogether comfortable with the lamb. His "proper animal," he says, is the cow. As a Jew and a secularist, he rejects the sentimental Christian imagery wherein Jesus is gentle and lamblike. Mention of the lamb makes the poem seem "serene and mystical," when what he intends is something "more primitive than Christianity, that violent thing which Christianity mollified."[7]

In "Picking the Roses" (*PP* 6–7), another poem that reenacts spring rituals, this "violent thing," both primitive and subconscious, is recapitulated and contained through ritual. The poem is also a major example of Stern's use of the eccentric speaker to interrupt and reinvent a conventional response to the garden. It begins in February, with a description of concrete action; the gardener-poet is involved in selection, one of his crucial duties. He is choosing plants from a catalog for the next life cycle and deciding where to place them:

> I am picking the roses for next time,
> Little Darlings for the side of the house,
> Tiffany and Lilli Marlene for the hot slope
> where the strawberries used to be.

The poem hints at its own wild destiny by mentioning a boar who might be "snorting" outside the house. He stands for the primitivity which always lurks outside our domestic enclosures. He may also contain a hint of prophecy, since in another poem the speaker snorts like a prophet (*RC* 86–87). The boar is necessary: "We will need him" for the vernal rite of blood sacrifice and rebirth, "the bleeding and regeneration to come." Here the poem moves into the future tense which it will sustain throughout.

The second stanza looks forward to planting. The "dead plants will arrive by mail," with "a leaf or two" to signal rebirth. The speaker is confident of his garden-wisdom, his poet-wisdom, which rests on a sense of timing:

> When the time comes I will walk outside to hear my name
> ring through the trees, or stop for a minute to hear the
> words skip
> on the water or collect like mice behind the garbage cans.

The name ringing in the trees contains many reverberations: the poet's calling or vocation, Stern's old longing for recognition, union with nature, echoes of God calling to Adam, to Abraham. At this signal he will be ready to plant: "I will tear the ground with my shovel. . . ." The shovel and the pen or pencil are Stern's signature implements; they unite the gardener and the poet, the making of the garden and the poem by an active protagonist.

The third stanza casts a mythic overlay on an everyday scene. The speaker imagines he will struggle with the boar in what we infer to be the completion of the blood sacrifice, a far more primitive and violent version of the rite than the lamb's version. It will occur on a neighborhood street and will not be seen but heard: "Then for two blocks up and two blocks down / my screams, and the screams of the boar, / will mix together." The man and the beast will be joined, complicitous. Afterward, there will be tearful talk "and touches of cynicism and histrionics / in the living rooms by the river," as if the struggle had been a family or neighborhood argument. This passage may well provide another example of the hidden incident which, though it might have instigated the poem, is almost completely elided in Stern, leaving subtextual pressure and subtle reverberations on the surface. In any case, the quotidian living rooms merge with a tribal scene as the stanza ends with a "crash of bone against bone, / mixture of broken weapons and falling shadows."

The long, final stanza contains the aftermath of rest and affirmation which the speaker will have earned through a struggle that will leave him scarred: "My poor left eye will be closed shut / behind its puffy hill / and my right thigh will be permanently twisted." He will sleep on his "mohair sofa"; he will rock in his "metal chair"; he will wait for spring renewal:

> I will collect all the stupidity and sorrow
> of the universe in one place
> and wait—like everyone else—
> for the first good signs,
> the stems to turn green,
> the buds to swell and redden,
> the clouds to fall, the trees to bend,
> the tenors of all 3,000 counties
> to tremble in the grass,

> to beat their chests, to tear their shirts,
> to stumble against the sopranos, to rise and fall
> like birds in the muddy grass,
> like heavy birds in last year's muddy grass.

This expansive ending is, in its sense, a typical romantic affirmation. But it's redeemed by strategies that interfere with the reader's easy glide into sentiment. The barest touch of self-parody, the unexpected infusion of humor in "the tenors of all 3,000 counties" who "stumble against the sopranos" undercuts the exalted statement just enough to save it from melodrama. The ending almost loses its footing, threatens to slip into comedy on one side or overstatement on the other, but manages a riveting balance till it lets us down gently into "last year's muddy grass."

Throughout the poem, conventional response is deterred by tactics that create density and complexity. Odd juxtapositions surprise us: convincing particulars, such as "lilies in plastic bags" with "roots like radishes," crash against wondrous occurrences. Elision complicates our reading; we react to much more than what appears: to the offstage contest with the boar and the primitive vision it elicits and to the suggested neighborhood scene. The abrupt splicing of these dramas, one mythic and fantastic, the other temporal and typical, defamiliarizes and heightens them both. It's one of Stern's favorite strategies, used to dissolve lineal time in recurring time. His favored future tense also complicates the temporal field, lifting the poem out of actuality into the exhilarating realm of possibility. And future tense provides the word *will*, with its implications of determination and desire; rebirth *will* happen because the speaker *wills* it.

In the speaker, these strategies are unified and embodied. They become more than mere tactics, like stage directions which become authentic in the genuine performance. The speaker confounds our expectations and goes on to suspend our disbelief. He's such an ordinary fellow, with his garden catalogs, his "towel against the front door / to keep the wind out," his back ache, his old sofa. Yet his encounters are extraordinary. You can't take your eyes off him for wondering what he'll do next, what he'll say next. He enjoins our faith in his adventure by sheer strength.

The country gardens discussed above thrive in a pastoral realm set apart from the urban twentieth century, like photographs which carefully exclude power lines and other signs of the present. Most country poems are like that; they look as if the city did not exist. And city poems ignore the country. Most poets—and even groups of poets—are identified with one *topos* or the other. City poets are usually pessimistic or deeply ironic; pastoral poets are accused of romantic irrelevance.

One of Stern's goals is to combine country and city in one vision, as Whitman does and, in a certain sense, Stevens does. Stern hopes to reopen an access to the pastoral myth by incorporating it in the present:

> Today as I ride down Twenty-fifth Street I smell honeysuckle
> rising from Shell and Victor Balata and K-Diner.
> The goddess of sweet memory is there
> staggering over fruit and drinking old blossoms.
> A man in white socks and a blue T-shirt
> is sitting on the grass outside Bethlehem Steel
> eating lunch and dreaming. (*RC* 44)

"One Foot in the River" (*LL* 5) defines the interpenetration of country and city as Stern knew it when he lived on the river in Raubsville, Pennsylvania, traveling often to the city: "Going to New York I carry the river in my head / and match it with the flow on 72nd Street and the flow on Broadway." The poet functions as a bridge: "one foot on 72nd Street, one foot in the river."

In an interview, Stern says that the separation between country and city myths is an illusion. Behind and underneath the city, with its neat grid of streets, its "reason and logic and order," is the country, "the unconscious, the past, the interior," with its "chaos and destruction and disorganization and timelessness and simplicity and primitivism and childishness" (Hillringhouse 26). This sounds more like the forest of legend than the bucolic village of pastoral, but the country scene of the poems is mostly rural and homey until it dissolves in myth or is blended with city life through the person of the gardener, who keeps "one knee in the tomatoes, / one knee on the cement" (*PP* 35).

Stern is impatient with those who reject the city. Their position is a "privileged" one, "reactionary and fake bucolic and sentimental," which stems from "our very hatred and fear of life and people and their things." He prefers to see the city as "a surrogate natural world" (Hillringhouse 27).

In "A Garden" (*L* 60–61), the natural world enters the city by way of "a piece of jade in a plastic cup, a bell jar / full of monarchs, a bottle of weeds, a Jew / hanging out of a glass, and one live flower, / a thin geranium in a jar of water." This windowsill garden is the speaker's "tulips," his "gory roses," his "hollyhock." He hopes his surrogate garden will provide some of the rewards of pastoral: "a little comfort," a "refuge / between the shells and the coffee can, some pleasure / among the red petals. . . ."[8]

"The Poem of Liberation" (*RC* 58–60) is the central example of Stern's use of the garden trope to explore urban issues. It begins with a comic association:

> The smell of piss is what we have in the city
> to remind us of the country and its dark ammonia.
> In the subway it's like a patch of new lilac
> or viburnum in the air . . .

The speaker wanders the city, as he does in many poems. New York's East Side reminds him of "the stone walls in Italy / or the tiny alleys behind the bazaars in Africa." In Stern, every city contains the ghosts of distant and ancient cities; his internationalism and historicism are among the features he shares with the high moderns.

The subject of the poem, discovered in his wanderings, is two gardens that stand across the street from one another in symbolic opposition. The first is a people's garden, overt, spontaneous, chaotic, practical, and profane; the second is a biblical garden, secret, ordered, symbolic, and holy.

The people's garden is "The Plaza Caribe," "planted in the rubble / of a wrecked apartment house." In spite of its vulgarity, it suggests spiritual rebirth: it seems to "claim the spirit" of the building back, "before it could be buried / in another investment of glass and cement." With its confused mixture of "thin maples and pieces of orange brick / and weeds and garbage as well as little rows / of beans and lettuce," with its "lush presence of objects" that are "crowded into the smallest space," it contains "the soul of New York."

Across the street is the unfinished St. John's Cathedral, with its "splintered doors" and "pile of rubbish." At the back, hidden from view, is "a biblical / fantasy of trees and herbs and flowers," arranged "in perfect clusters" with plants from various books of the Bible.

The people's garden is one of the neglected places that attract Stern; they are inaccessible, not to people who frequent them, but to the culture. Though in clear view, they are culturally hidden, invisible: they are below notice. In an essay, he calls them "melancholy pockets." He describes a hillside near the East Liberty station outside Pittsburgh: "There were no trees on the hill, just cheap grass, yellow dirt, broken glass and weeds." He remembers a woman picking weeds there, a goddess of the hillside. Though he admits the sexist implications of his image, he identifies her with, among other things, "commitment to the heart," "concordance with nature," "sensuality," "concrete knowledge," and "fear of machines." Against her he posits a man looking down on the woman from a "hideous aluminum or stainless steel building." He is "the god at the window," who stands for qualities that include "addiction to logic," "dependence on technology," "efficiency," "uniformity," "ruthlessness," and "denial" ("Notes" 12.3: 42–43). The woman picking weeds, her junk-strewn hillside, and the people's garden all represent a pastoral of the demos, an Edenic vision reborn in urban America.

The two gardens in "Poem of Liberation" are both art objects, though only the church garden is intended as such. They represent two aesthetics, two kinds of artistic significance: that of the cloistered, aristocratic, High Church, which is traditional, literary, and formal, and that of the people, which is revolutionary and vigorous and admits the accidental.

These gardens also compare in a most provocative way with the two kinds of cities described by Gerald L. Bruns in *Cain: Or, the Metaphorical Construction of Cities*. The church garden fits the traditional idea of polis, a patterned, reasoned, powerful, rule-governed, fixed container, with an official language. The people's garden belongs to the labyrinthian city, heteroglossic crossroad of the wanderer, the exile, the migrant, the lawless, the powerless, the random, the anonymous—the vernacular city that is "always out of control—always going to pieces and reforming . . . according to no law or principle" (85 and *passim*).

Yet Stern's two gardens aren't as distinct as one would expect, since the secular garden contains intimations of burial and rebirth that should belong to the church, while the church garden is hedged by rubble and disrepair. The church garden is not "a sacred version of the profane," nor is the people's garden a "vile parody of the other." The Stern speaker wishes to "like one garden and hate the other," but finds himself "loving both, both ideas, / both deeply thought out, both passionate" (RC 59–60).

The tension between high and low culture, the academy and the streets, is seen often in Stern. In "The Picasso Poem" (RC 80–82), the speaker visits the Museum of Modern Art. While waiting to "crawl through the numbered rooms," he imagines a drive on the Pulaski Skyway. He can't decide between Fifth Avenue and the sulphurous "Jersey swamp": "I waver between / that world and this. I travel back and forth / between the two."

"The Poem of Liberation" continues as the speaker leaves the church garden, after resting "under the olive trees" in the old calm of symmetry and certainty. He spends his "last hour" reading "the poem of liberation—in Spanish and English—nailed up on the wire fence." He walks "through the Plaza Caribe / under the slogans and the brown faces," thinking of the similarity between Jewish and Spanish sorrow: "Hebrew melancholy and Moorish wailing. . . ." He realizes that it's not another instance of oversimplified idealism, "that other bitter stupid dream again"; instead, "it's hope mixed in with memory. . . ."[9] This typical unexplained *it* may be the people's garden, the poem on the fence, the scene in the Plaza Caribe, the poem he's writing, or all of these.

The poem moves into a series of ruminations that lead to enactment of the speaker's familiar garden ritual: "I dig a hole in the ground / and pour in my mixture of meal and water. / I spread the roots out in three directions / and pack them in with dirt." These ceremonious gestures provide a synthesis of the poem's materials that is intuitive and musical rather than logical. The speaker is ready to move on, away from us, carrying his ritual implement, the "small steel shovel / humming and singing in the blue dust."

The junk and weeds seen in "The Poem of Liberation" crop up throughout Stern. He says that he discovered in his own poems "an obsession with small animals and neglected things, weeds, overlooked things that people either pick on or drive over" and, by extension, to overlooked parts of the world and "invisible people." This kind of emphasis stems, he says, from pity for your own childhood: "I was neglected . . . spiritually and psychologically abandoned" (Glaser 23). Here he refers to the childhood incident

that instigated his central fantasy: his sister's death and the conse-
quent loss of his parents as they turned away from him toward their
own grief. He was, in a sense, exiled from the family, cast from the
paradise of childhood. Later, when he was rejected as a young poet
—barred from the family of poets, as it were—his position as out-
cast was corroborated.

Junk and weeds are emblems of the ruined world: they represent
the exile, the forsaken. When Stern accommodates ruin in his con-
temporary pastoral, he makes room for the stranger. Weeds are
"stragglers and drifters" (*R* 74) admired for their "stubbornness and
secrecy" (*R* 28), qualities the poet has identified as his own ("Some
Secrets" 265).[10] Images of detritus infuse his nature imagery with
anti-aristocratic vigor, participating in the reimagined pastoral
where lilacs collide with "broken cinder blocks," "bicycle tires," "old
weeds and power lines" (*R* 23). The speaker finds sorrow and re-
pentance in "the broken glass / and the old pile of chair legs," "the
old shoes, / and the daisies" (*R* 32–33). He could spend ten years
"bringing the things together": "ten good years on the river / watch-
ing the spars and the starved deer and the bathtubs float by" (*R* 39).
Stern asks us to view our American ruins with the same respect we
pay to the ruins of antiquity. Our "mound of dirt" and "broken tele-
phone booth" are as valid as the Greek remnants we treasure: "give
me anything, a pebble from the Agora, a tile from Phaistos; / and
here is a perfectly intact bottle of Bollo." We should visit the junk-
yard like tourists, and "walk gently over the broken glass . . ." (*LL*
64–65).

Stern also associates refuse with the ruin of American poetry in
the modern age. In one of his essays, he discusses the burial of po-
etry in the rubble of technology: "Technology destroyed the past, it
ruined continuity," especially in America where the only history is
imported. In 1910 or 1920, he believes, we crossed a threshold
where "the feeling of irreparable loss" and the impossibility of "true
renewal" began to dominate. This "loss of will" led to a retreat into
issues of style: "artistic newness" was confused with the heroic. The
great technical breakthrough produced "magnificent poetry," but it
was also a dislocation of feeling ("Notes" 12.1: 21). Stern sees him-
self as "the strange man / who has moved into the ruin" (*R* 40).

Stern's identification with the stranger has much to do with his
Jewish identity. Jews were not allowed to own land; they were ex-
iled from the countryside, yet attacked for not understanding

flowers.[11] In "Gold Flower" (LL 49), the Stern speaker explains that the garden is his "new worship." He "had walked through gardens all [his] life without seeing them." With comic irony, he praises the "dear world of strangers," Christian America, his hosts, the planters of flowers in whose house he is an alien. The Jew is "a guest in his own garden" (LL 31).

In "Peace in the Near East" (LL 31–32), birds nest in the speaker's garden, "carrying twigs and paper and leaves and straw / back and forth. . . ." They are "building the Aswan Dam out there." Soon they will be "greeting the Arabian ambassador on the right, / greeting the Russian ambassador on the left,

> and finally even the Jew himself, a guest
> in his own garden, a holder of strange credentials,
> one who is permitted to go through the carrots
> only with special consent, one who is scolded
> if he gets too close to the raspberry bushes

The Jew's own garden, here, is the State of Israel, but also all the gardens where he has been denied access. Beneath them all is the original garden from which he was barred as Adam.

Stern uses the black locust tree, sometimes called yellow locust or acacia, as a symbol of himself as Jew; it's a tree, he has said, that grows where nothing else will.[12] He explains its significance in an interview:

> My identity with that tree has something to do with Judaism and with persecution. The tree is short-lived—forty years maybe—it's asymmetrical, considered ugly, worthless. Farmers value it only as a source of fence posts. People, when they buy land, chop them down to replace them with shade trees—I love that tree, I identify with it; it's my poverty tree. I sometimes see the concentration camp number on the forearm, or forelimb. (Hillringhouse 27)

The locust is a suitable choice for a Jewish tree, since its name also stands for one of the plagues visited on the Egyptians. In "Four Sad Poems on the Delaware" (LL 24–25) Stern's spokesman depicts himself as this tree:

This is a locust tree, dying of love,
waiting one more time for its flowers to come,
regretting its life on the stupid river,
growing more and more Jewish as its limbs weaken.

Sometimes a birch tree takes the place of a locust. In "I Slept Like That" (*L* 24), the speaker insists he "was always a birch tree, / with a long curved bough and a limb hanging down / half touching the grass": "I slept by the river—always—and followed the devious way. / In five old cities, each with an ancient and brutal government, / I lived with my arm in the sky and my fingers bent."

"Acacia" (*RC* 62) is Stern's main tract on the locust. The tree is used to pull together an array of materials, from a cathedral in Albi to the lobby of a Howard Johnson's full of baby lambs and fresh flowers. The locust stands not only for the Jews but for all the displaced, the alien, the wanderer, the survivor: "In locust trees the roots run along the ground / and bury themselves in the sides of hills for survival." They don't have their own place, but must "grow in roses and strawberries." Competing theories about the tree's origins are introduced in the poem. The speaker says it "came from western Pennsylvania / and was brought to Europe in the nineteenth century." A friend believes it is "now French but originally / it grew in southern China and India." Further on, the speaker declares that it was "in the Allegheny mountains / where locusts first started, four million years ago." The locust's story enters the myth of the stranger, the wanderer whose origins are always somewhere else—the outcast who has been deprived of his habitation, the weed forced to survive outside the garden.

The gardener is the core role of the Stern speaker, representative of the first place, the initial story. He unifies earth and myth. A down-to-earth, neighborhood gardener who likes to give advice, he is also a fantast whose vision encompasses origins, exile, and reconciliation. Other Stern spokesmen, the wanderer, the rabbi, and the angel manifest later aspects of the biblical myth. They are not distinct from him but join him in one characterization that binds the poems together.

The garden speaker portrays both the receptive role of repose and the authoritative role of action. Both are significant in Stern, but the strong role is far more compelling. The strong figure is mature and patriarchal. Neither tenuous nor uncertain, he is teacher, guiding spirit, and intercessor in his ritual domain. He answers a need in today's poetry for a voice of authority; his strong stance is acceptable because it is moderated by humility, playfulness, and kindliness, and because it is based on active participation.

The strong role is especially crucial in the garden poems. It overcomes an extreme tendency toward the bucolic banal which has become inherent in the garden trope. This bleached response is a symptom of our thirst for a redeemed myth of the garden. History has replaced myth, under the aegis of lineality. But we're bored with history; the only way to escape it is to reenter ideal time. Stern's hero keeps one foot in the world and the other in myth, demonstrating that history is folded in recurrence. His determination to reappropriate debased symbols is a sign of strength; his verbal sleight-of-hand brings the reader into renewed dialogue with the garden. In his *muthos*, it is not a distant landscape but a contemporary terrain that incorporates the past, not a pretty, innocuous garden but a passionate, even brutal one. The syntax of the garden is a syntax of life and death:

> for the poet bent over his rows
> digging up huge chunks of dirt,
> bowing and dancing like a white pigeon on Spring Street,
> singing again about buried love and crazy renewal. (*RC* 51)

→IV←

Here I Am Walking

The Stern poem is a quest and lesson rooted steadfastly in the Bible. Important roles of the Stern speaker reflect the spiritual history portrayed there, from the Creation and Fall, represented by the gardener, to death and rebirth, ruled by the trope of the angel. The life span between these extremes of experience is governed by the wanderer and the rabbi. More than roles, these stances are conflicting tendencies and ideas that underlie all of Stern and sometimes emerge in characters. They represent opposed paradigms of the quest for significance and sanction, and opposed views of meaning itself: the quest and meaning of the stranger against that of the native, the rootless against the fixed, the guest against the host, the rebel against the elect, the accidental against the coherent, the labyrinth against the grid, revolution against tradition, prophecy against fulfillment. The quest and meaning of the stranger is an experiment, while that of the native is doctrinal. Their opposition expresses the foundation of narrative: disruption versus stasis. In the Bible, the contest between these forces is portrayed in the largest possible arena.

The Bible is, in several ways, a crucial aesthetic model for Stern. It uses history to create vision, as does his enterprise. It mixes wisdom and prophecy, a combination Stern admires and emulates throughout the corpus. And no doubt he admires it as a model for the dramatization of ideas. Even more important is a drive in Stern which draws him not to the middle ground but to the core, to the first source, the magnificent authority, the huge themes. He is drawn also not to the periphera but to the edge, the excessive, the extreme—and the Bible is the most extreme of books. To be influenced by the Bible is to be under the influence of God himself and to become, thereby, a prophet.

Stern's biblical inclinations are immediately obvious in the ring of his work. The poet's familiarity with the Bible stems from having been raised in a strong Jewish tradition. The influence of Judaism itself, he says, has been "a little tenuous and sometimes nostalgic." But "the historical idea of the Jew as an eternally stubborn, hopeful, and dreaming creature has been an influence . . . " ("Some Secrets" 256–57). And Jewish culture has an especial appeal: "I love its crazy combinations, I admire its joy and optimism, its love of the mind, its hatred of violence, its acceptance of life, its sensuousness, its music" (Hillringhouse 30). This summary could pass as a description of his own work; we might add other qualities identified with Jewish life and seen in his writing, such as joyful sorrow, faith in the past, and devotion to learnedness.

His religious upbringing provided an affinity for the Bible which is internalized and partly unconscious. It shows up not only in rhythm and phrasing but also in wording. He likes to recount how an audience member once told him, after a reading, that "my goings out / and my comings in," a phrase in "The Rose Warehouse" (RC 66), is from the morning service. He had not been aware of the source (Hillringhouse 30; Pinsker 61).

Many of his biblical allusions are, however, quite deliberate, as are references to the kabbalistic and Hassidic traditions. A key example is the red coal which he takes as title for a poem and also a book. Stern's recapitulation of this figure takes us back through Shelley to biblical sources. One of these is the passage in Isaiah where a seraphim lays a live coal on the mouth of the prophet to cleanse him of sin. He is thus prepared to take God's message to the people and says, "Here am I, send me" (6: 6–9). Another source is the Hassidic image of "sparks" as fallen bits of divine light that long to rejoin God. A more significant source for Stern is the Moses story as reimagined by Midrash Ex. 1: 26.[1] Here, the three-year-old Moses plucks the Pharaoh's crown from his head. The ruler tests the child's motives by placing gems and hot coals before him. Moses reaches for the gems, that is, for the emblem of Pharaoh's power, but the angel Gabriel saves him by guiding his hand to the coals. As a result, Moses becomes tongue-tied. This story seems to warn that reaching for another's glory can damage your speech, a particular danger for the poet.

Stern's "The Red Coal" (*RC* 68–69) is, among other things, a subtle and perhaps partly unconscious response to the Moses story. It refers to the photograph of Stern and his friend Jack Gilbert which is used on the cover of the book. The speaker-poet thinks of placing the photo beside one of Pound and Williams, "to see what coals had done to their lives too." It seems that he wants to place his friend and himself in majestic company, to put the two photos on the same shelf. He assures us that he speaks of Pound and Williams "with vast affection, / wanting desperately to know what the two of them talked about," in Pennsylvania and later at St. Elizabeth's, "the suffering finally taking over their lives." He apparently wants to be on intimate terms with these forbears. The poem goes on to compare Gilbert's early fame with Stern's obscurity. It speaks of "how we now carry the future with us": "The coal has taken over, the red coal / is burning between us and we are at its mercy— / as if a power is finally dominating / the two of us . . . as if knowledge is what we needed and now / we have that knowledge." The coal exemplifies Stern's preference for natural and universal symbols. Here, it is amorphous, connected to knowledge, power, memory, inspiration, and poetry itself. This is one of a few poems in the corpus where the speaker is virtually identical to Stern himself; autobiography dominates, and in my view, the poem suffers for it. The burning coal was on Stern's mind much earlier; in a poem from *Rejoicings*, he defines it as poetry: the poet's call is to "free the living coals" and "feed the flame" (*R* 67).

The kabbalistic and Hassidic interpretations of Torah are more likely to be sources for Stern than the liturgy, because ultimately he is more interested in mythic memory than social memory. However, he notes that he uses these mystical texts as "a kind of midwife and secret metaphor for my own inclinations" ("Some Secrets" 256–57). His interest in Hassidism goes beyond the sect formed in eighteenth-century Poland to its ancient roots in the folkways of the Palestinian tribes.[2] Hassidism appeals to Stern because it is a tradition of practice, not of law, and is associated with archaic functions of poetry: mediation between God and humanity, the gift of prophecy, the transformation of matter into spirit. It can be seen as a democratization of the same mystical tradition which in the kabbala takes a scholarly form. Kabbalism is crucial for Stern because it purports to come out of a secret oral tradition older than Judaism itself, supposedly reflected in a network of hidden metaphors in the Pentateuch. The concept of the secret text is central in Stern. He is pleased by the kabbala's potent, transgressing interpretations of Torah and by the idea of a parallel, unofficial version more powerful than the doctrinal one.

"Blue Skies, White Breasts, Green Trees" (*LL* 27–28) is a reflection on the vagaries of imagination that demonstrates Stern's uses of kabbala:

What I took to be a man in a white beard
turned out to be a woman in a silk babushka
weeping in the front seat of her car;
and what I took to be a seven-branched candelabrum
with the wax dripping over the edges
turned out to be a horse's skull
with its teeth sticking out of the sockets.
It was my brain fooling me,
sending me false images,
turning crows into leaves
and corpses into bottles,
and it was my brain that betrayed me completely,
sending me entirely uncoded material,
for what I thought was a soggy newspaper
turned out to be the first Book of Concealment, written in
    English,
and what I thought was a grasshopper on the windshield
turned out to be the Faithful Shepherd chewing blood,
and what I thought was, finally, the real hand of God
turned out to be only a guy wire and a
pair of broken sunglasses.

Here, official religious symbols stem from corrupt imagination, which invents a Godlike "man in a white beard." Perception is useless; it sees what is actually death, a horse's skull, as an emblem of faith, a Menorah. The hand of God, a background icon for Stern's profuse imagery of hands, turns out to be only a pair of glasses hanging on a wire. Valid spiritual messages, on the other hand, go unnoticed: *The Book of Concealment* is taken for a wet newspaper and *The Faithful Shepherd* is dismissed as a dead grasshopper. These are two interpolated commentaries on Exodus found in the Zohar, or *Book of Splendor,* the central kabbalistic document. They are hidden meanings that appear in metaphoric disguise, as they do in the poem. The fact that these texts buried in the Stern text are comments both on and in the Zohar, another text which is itself a mystical commentary or "hidden midrash" on the text of Exodus, conveys us through a sea of intertextuality to the exile. The fall into consciousness is the source of the quandary in the poem, where the brain *betrays* the speaker. By hooking his own poem onto the chain of textual commentary, he enters the secret tradition.

As the poem continues, the speaker resolves to avoid the misapprehensions of imagination; he will "reverse everything" and take action in the real world: "I am ready to take the woman with the white scarf / in my arms and stop her moaning, / and I am ready to light the horse's teeth, / and I am ready to stroke the dry leaves." Ironically, the woman, the horse's skull, and the leaves, the supposed "correct" interpretations of reality, are as much images as the mistaken ones. And the speaker confuses the two when he proposes to light the horse's teeth as if it were in fact a Menorah. There is, of course, no way out of the impasse; nonetheless, will and action are favored over passivity, as is spiritual preparation, being *ready.*

Beyond the intertextuality among the mystical texts, they are part of a universal *histos* of signification. Correspondences have been found between kabbala and the old religions of Akkadia, India, China, and Egypt as well as Platonism and neo-Platonism, Aristotelian thought, and Christian Gnosticism. Stern even sees an "insane connection" between Hassidism and Zen. He jokes about his belated discovery that the sitting he does so much of in his poems is related to both: "People in both movements sit a lot. . . . I now discover that, all this time, I was involved in a religious ritual" (Glaser 28). The universal aspect of the mystical texts is central to their importance for Stern. They appeal to him because they represent the hidden, common core—the undertext, as it were, of the human attempt to define spirit.

This undertext is not the canon of the rabbi but the heterodoxy of the wanderer, the stranger, an old and omnipresent character whose trope goes back to Cain and up to, for instance, *The Invisible Man.* Whenever he appears, he recalls the eviction; his wandering is the consequence of his fall into knowledge. He prizes his consciousness but is also nostalgic and sometimes wishes to lose it, to stop wandering. His trope encompasses a range of meanings, but he is always excluded from a system that is, for some reason, unattainable or unacceptable. He may be an outcast, a rebel, or a mystic whose exile is self-imposed. His assumptions don't match those of the realm. Because he is not a participant, he can see clearly. Because he is outside the establishment, he identifies with the powerless. He may be a sacrificial figure, rejected because he represents a critique of society's values. Or he may be seduced by a corrupt society. Or he may evict himself from ordinary life into a testing ground. After his trial, he may return as prophet.[3] His dream of change takes its ultimate form in the imagery of rebirth.

The stranger reflects Stern's fantasy of alienation, which comes out of eviction from the family and long exclusion from the poet's community. The rabbi manifests his goal of acceptance as an authority figure. This dualism finds expression in his admiration for the experimental, chancy, and vigorous on one side, the formal and traditional on the other. It is resolved in the myth of himself as an exile who returns as prophet. He has said that the subject of his early work was "the regeneration and transformation of the world, and myself as religio-politico-linguistic hero, a common enough theme for a first generation American Jew only son" ("Some Secrets" 261). Indeed, it is often called the definitive theme of modernism. But for Stern it is inherent and inevitable; like a tune that must be played, it modulates endlessly in his work.

The stranger's modus operandi is wandering, or traveling without a map: a way to seek meanings off accepted paths. Discursive and intuitive, wandering invites serendipity, and serendipity creates significance; a meaning discovered this way seems more important than would the same one discovered in expected channels. "Going off the track" can also be a way to defer meaning, enhancing its value. Meaning may sometimes be forestalled because it is both desired and feared, creating the opposition between going forth and holding back that Beckett calls "push-pull"; we recognize it as a standard device of narrative.

Wandering is, of course, the method of the Stern poem, a method which is a statement about meaning: meaning is the *to be found*. Writing is not an instrument used to convey the known but a procedure used to discover the unknown. The terminology of Roland Barthes is tempting in this regard; we might call Stern's text "writerly" as opposed to "readerly." Readerly texts are static and consoling; they uphold an orthodox view of meaning. Writerly texts call the reader to collaborate in an unsettling, even dangerous excursion toward an unknown destination. However, Barthes, in a move close to that of abstract painting, calls for "intransitive" writing meant to produce only itself. This retreat from reference stems from the dread of sentiment. Ultimately, it says that the world outside the text, the human world, is beyond hope. The interplay between Barthes and Stern breaks off at the word *instrument*; Barthes wants a noninstrumental writing; Stern chooses an instrument played without a score but nonetheless meant to serve a purpose beyond its own music (*S/Z* 4; "To Write" 144). And besides, the fact is that there's a schism between Stern's method and his meaning: the unknown meaning he finds off the familiar path turns out to be an old one, traditional and comforting. But it's renewed by the process in which it is sought and by its position as *the found*.

The nexus of method and meaning in Stern is, of course, the speaker. It is he, a fumbling, uncertain, yet determined human representative, who confronts the unknown in the process of his adventure. Stern comments on the function of the speaker's quest in a reflection on the poem "Sycamore" which applies to all his work:

> What gives it tension and complexity, what makes it, in its own way, significant or original, or mysterious, what makes it moving—if it is that—is the presence of the narrator in the very middle of what is to him an overwhelming and confusing and complicated experience which he can never fully comprehend, which has hold of him in spite of his peaceful and knowledgeable mode and which he can only partially make sense of, and control, through a dutiful and almost domestic use of those myths and rites. ("'Sycamore': Poem and Commentary" 5)

This method is not a mere device; the struggle is authentic. It is Stern's struggle, as he explains:

> I speak of "him" and the "narrator" as if I were talking of someone else's experience. The fact is that it was I who was the center of both the poem and the experience, and it was an experience that was overwhelming and complicated and confusing to me. . . . (5)

Here I Am Walking

In the poem, Stern loses—or is willing to surrender—control: "I am to a significant degree being acted upon, I am an agent, I am almost a victim, rather than a 'creator' in the Blakean sense of the word." He believes, interestingly, that the poem is successful to the degree that he is unable to control it (6). In this he refers, perhaps, to a certain roughness or unruly quality in the strong poem which contrasts with the smooth, facile, "perfect" poem. In another sense, his comment reflects the mystical position where surrender leads to a more serious and potent kind of dominion than what was relinquished. Overall, his work values both the exercise of will and the surrender of control, compatible halves of a single drama in which he is both actor and agent.

One of Stern's most necessary statements of the poet's role is "Making the Light Come" (*L* 52). The title carries the quality of agency, that which makes something happen, as well as implications of the artist as maker. The poem is framed by the speaker's two favorite implements: it begins with a description of a fountain pen with "stripes / of gold or silver at the shaft for streaks / of thought and feeling" and ends with the gardener's spade. It contrasts two ways of seeking the light; the first was the speaker's way "three dozen years ago," which was strained and outward facing:

> I turned my face to the light—a frog does that,
> not only a bird—and changed my metal table
> three or four times. I struggled for rights to the sun
> not only because of the heat. I wanted to see
> the shadows on the wall, the trees and vines,
> and I wanted to see the white wisteria
> hanging from the roof. To sit half under it,
> Light was my information. . . .

One of the significant items in this passage is the substitution of *information* for *inspiration*: light is here a source of data rather than of vision. The words *struggled* and *rights* are also key; they point to a misdirected effort to claim a privilege. This approach to light

> led me
> astray, I never saw it was a flower
> and darkness was the seed; I never potted
> the dirt and poured the nutriments, I never

> waited week after week for the smallest gleam.
> I sit in the sun forgiving myself; I know
> exactly where to dig. What other poet
> is on his knees in the frozen clay with a spade
> and a silver fork, fighting the old maples,
> scattering handfuls of gypsum and moss, still worshiping?

Here, in a typical Sternian—and mystical—dualism, light must be sought in the dark. Vision requires patience. It calls for an informed participation; one must prepare for it by "potting the dirt" and "pouring the nutriments." In his mistaken approach, the speaker kept moving his table, changing his position or perspective. In his valid effort, he knows "exactly where to dig." Though he is not physically passive, his state of mind is open and receptive, worshipful rather than demanding. As the posture of both prayer and gardening, "on his knees" joins the two sides of the dichotomy.

In many poems, the Stern speaker does not know "exactly where to dig," but he knows a way of finding his place by combining the will to go forth with a surrender to the unpredictable. This method is materialized in the role of the speaker as wandering Jew, wandering poet, a seeker and guide who embodies both process and theme. When the speaker walks, he is making his way through the action of the poem and also through the writing of it. A common setting is the seashore, a wandering track that provides a romantic setting for the onset of prophecy.

In "Here I Am Walking" (*RC* 86–87), the speaker begins typically by pointing himself out and naming his location:

> Here I am walking between Ocean and Neptune,
> sinking my feet in mile after mile of wet life.
> I am practically invisible
> in the face of all this clutter,

The clutter that makes him invisible is the crowded beach scene on one level and the crowded poem—or the materials that cry out for admission to the poem—on another. Here and in many poems, wandering leads to the discovery of a meditative place where the speaker does the "sitting" identified with Zen and the Hassidic tradition; he will "sit on the black rocks / to make my connections" and study the residue of the past, "the footprints going in and out of the water." He will "dream up a small blue god to talk to." He imagines himself "snorting like a prophet" and "living in dreams."

Another setting where the wanderer sometimes appears is the garden. His appearance here plays directly on the eviction, but he may also enact other themes. We have already seen him in "The Poem of Liberation" (*RC* 58–61), where a people's garden and a doctrinal church garden are discovered fortuitously on a typical city walk.[4] These gardens are spatial figures for the dichotomy of the wanderer and the rabbi.

"No Longer Terror" (*L* 62–64) is a garden poem where wandering and sitting represent a "push-pull" movement between world and thought, a gesture that goes out and back, out and back, that moves toward, then defers, acceptance of death. When the speaker says, "I start to wander again," he means he is beginning the discursive journey of another poem, as well as its action: he wants to wander to the hills and back "before it's dark." Throughout the sensuous garden imagery of the poem, with its complex themes, its Orphic allusions, its light, dark, and shadow, the speaker keeps us with him by reminding us, in his usual way, of his movements and position: "I sit," "I walk inside," "I will look," "I will go back to my chair," "I'll wait," "I'll wait," "I'll wait," "I will walk out again," "I will just sit there," "I leave my chair," "the last thing I see," "the last thing I see," "the last thing I'll do," "the last thing I'll do." He is typically clumsy: "I stumble over / a plant and a table, I bang my knee on a trunk, / I trip on a rug." He seems nervous as he thinks about last things, about life and death: "thinking about the light, / how long it stayed, how long I will be in darkness. . . ."

As seen above, the movements of the speaker provide spatiotemporal orientation; he is what we hold onto for balance. In some poems, his footsteps create only an illusion of coherence, since they transgress time and space. In many cases, however, they record an actual walk that can be mapped.

"There I Was One Day" (*L* 26–27) is a ramble through Easton, Pennsylvania, that starts "In the parking lot of the First Brothers Church" and is held in place by orienting phrases: "there I was," "I stopped between," "I turned left," "we sat there," "later we left," and "doing a circle, east on one street, / north on another, past the round oak table / in the glass window, past the swimming pool / at the YW." References like these are rarely made up; there is something reassuring about their factual presence. In this framework, the speaker dramatizes reflections on ancestry, memories of childhood bitterness and anger, and social comment on the "pure decadence" of America, which he traces "to either Frank Sinatra or Jackie Gleason." The poem is made odd and comic by the fact that the speaker throughout is a bird, "a giant whooping crane" of international origins who has to stand on one foot:

> Just a walk for me
> is full of exhaustion; nobody does it my way,
> shaking the left foot, holding the right foot up,
> a stork from Broadway, a heron from Mexico,
> a pink flamingo from Greece.

When he says, "nobody does it my way," he speaks not only of his one-legged stance but also of his poem; it too is often a tiring walk.

Though he's seen in a variety of settings and themes, the conspicuous role of Stern's wanderer is exploration of American culture, which he views from a moving perspective rather than a rooted one. He looks "for wisdom / in the cold schools and the empty gas stations": "I wear my old blue necktie / and fly low like a frozen jay looking for happiness / in the slippery roads and the silent covered faces" (*LL* 33).

In "Going North on 202" (*R* 25), the speaker's discovery of America is compared with that of Christopher Columbus. As the poem opens, the speaker is caught in a traffic jam which stands for American life. The people are sacrificial lambs fighting their way through the traffic circle at Flemington, New Jersey, a "great circle" which suggests Dante's Hell.

> Going north on 202 I have to wait for hours
> for the American lambs to pass by.
> Thousands, thousands, crossing the great circle
>   at Flemington,
> more thousands coming up the road from Frenchtown,
> the meat juices running down their lips,
> their undersides stained with excrement,
> their hooves bloody from fighting.

These lines call to mind the crowds from Dante who flow over London Bridge in *The Waste Land*.

Here I Am Walking

After he gets on route 78, the Stern speaker passes Columbus, who is "looking for the Hudson" with a cross rattling at the car window and frightened chickens screaming in the back seat. Stern was thinking here of the chickens Castro butchered and ate during his stay at a Harlem hotel in the late 1950s.[5] The Columbus in the poem, however, is not a revolutionary wanderer but an orthodox one whose travels are sponsored by the realm. His discovery of America is the mistaken European one which long controlled—and still influences—America's view of itself. He is "going the other way," that is, backwards, toward Europe, a conservative, aristocratic little place preserved in mothballs:

> with its bishops smiling happily,
> with its daydreaming kings scratching their stomachs,
> with its donkey races, and its monsters, and its bells,
> tiny Europe waits for him,
> tiny Europe, smelling of camphor.

In "Lucky Life" (LL 43–45), Columbus appears as a statue, an official emblem. The scene is a summer beach, but the speaker dreams he is wandering, "walking through Phillipsburg, New Jersey." As often happens, he is lost: confused, abandoned, and fallen. He's trying to remember "which statue of Christopher Columbus / I have to look for":

> the one with him slumped over
> and lost in weariness or the one with him
> vaguely guiding the way with a cross and globe in
> one hand and a compass in the other.

Sources of direction such as the cross, map, and compass provide only vague guidance; they are symbols of orthodoxy and planned movement unsuitable for the wanderer's quest. He turns instead, in dream, to "sitting at the oak bar" of "the Eagle Hotel on Chamber Street" or "on the side porch." His nostalgic dream ends and the voice of the poem turns, becoming urgent and prayerful as it swings into the long, closing litany of "Lucky Life" which is Stern's most famous affirmation.

The wanderer goes forth courageously without a destination, moved by emotion. His fortunate arrivals—in the world and in the poem—are unexpected blessings. The Stern speaker makes this clear in "This Is It" (*LL* 59–61): "It is my emotions that carry me through Lambertville, New Jersey, / sheer feeling—and an obscure detour—that brings me to a coffee shop / called 'This Is It.'" His delight at finding a place with such a name leads him to feel that the world is collaborating in his poem: "Everyone is into my myth! The whole countryside / is studying weeds, collecting sadness, dreaming / of odd connections. . . ." It is on the serendipitous course of a detour that world and myth cohere.

Lambertville becomes an emblem of sadness, of the American tragedy. It is "a dream-ridden carcass where people live out serious lives / with other people's secrets. . . ." Sometimes they become wanderers in search of significance; they "leave the papers on the front porch" to walk through a typical American scene, "past abandoned factories and wooden garages, past the cannon with balls and the new band shell. . . ." But they end up in "stinking New Hope" (another fortunate name), where "all their deep longing / is reduced to an hour and a half of greedy buying." The speaker sits in "This Is It," a tar paper café that epitomizes a certain kind of American despair, and studies its "strange spirit," the spirit of materialism, as he waits "for the summer to bring its reckoning." In waiting for the *reckoning*, he is waiting for his check and also for the price to be paid for "greedy buying," only a sop to spiritual hunger.

Meditative pauses, the knots or clots in the speaker's wanderings, often occur in seedy restaurants. They are outsiders' places, sites of the people's culture that coexists with high culture in the corpus. He loves "The Way We Were Lounge," with its "broken notes" and "tilted cocktail glass" (*RC* 72); the "Cup and Saucer," where "heavy men . . . bend quietly over their eggs and bread" (*R* 76); and Bickford's, where he can rest among "the cracked cups and the corn muffins" and "let any beliefs that want to overtake me" (*LL* 3–4).

"There Is Wind, There Are Matches" (*RC* 70–71) is the major restaurant meditation of the Stern corpus; it contains prophecy, reconciliation of the past, and final accord. It opens as the speaker explains his restaurant habit: "A thousand times I have sat in restaurant windows, / through mopping after mopping, letting the ammonia clear / my brain and the music from the kitchens / ruin my heart." Today he's in Horn and Hardart's; it becomes the last place left in a doomed world. It becomes the world itself, "this place," which is dark and dry, bereft of spirit, ready to go up in flames:

> This is the last place left and everyone here
> knows it; if the lights were turned down, if the
> heat were turned off, if the banging of dishes stopped,
> we would all go on, at least for a while, but then
> we would drift off one by one toward Locust or Pine.
> —I feel this place is like a birch forest
> about to go; there is wind, there are matches, there is
> > snow,
> and it has been dark and dry for hundreds of years.

The speaker looks back on his life—on Stern's life—and decides it was not wasted. He can "leave this place without bitterness / and start my walk down Broad Street past the churches / and the tiny parking lots and the thrift stores." As he resumes his wanderings, he enjoys the epiphanic experience common in Stern; he unites with other lives—or rather, he enacts that transformation:

> I do the child sitting for his dessert,
> I do the poet asleep at his table,
> waiting for the sun to light up his forehead.
> I suddenly remember every ruined life,
> every betrayal, every desolation,
> as I walk past Tasker toward the city of Baltimore,
> banging my pencil on the iron fences,
> whistling Bach and Muczynski through the closed blinds.

Restaurants are among the secret enclosures, some of which he calls "pockets" and others "caves," that appeal to Stern; not necessarily hidden from view, they go unnoticed because they lie off the usual paths. Both figures represent the enclosed, womblike side of the poet's opposition between hidden and open, subconscious and conscious. The pocket is a hiding place from which one looks out; the cave is a place of reflection, a container for memory, a site for *gnosis*. Stern's own caves, hideaways like the "ancient cellar" of a house in Philadelphia or a room above an Army Navy store, remind him of Virgil's descent "through a wide-mouthed cavern," "St. Jerome in his dim grotto," "Don Quixote waiting to be lowered into Montesino's cave," "the cistern where Jeremiah ranted," "the cavity in God's brain where the virgin lay," "the collective unconscious of Jung," "the electric corridors of Ludwig II," and "Zeus himself," who was born in a cave. When Plato rejected the cave, Stern notes, he rejected poetry. For those who have no caves, there is "no sacred life, and no language" ("Notes" 16.3: 41–42, 45–46).

Caves and pockets are also secret aspects of a text, like the hidden meanings of the Pentateuch purportedly unveiled by the kabbala. Both are in fact references to an aspect of Stern's own text—and of his behavior in the text—that often goes unnoticed. Frederick Garber comments on a tension between Stern's overt and exuberant stance and a less obvious "language of the hidden," which "cannot come fully into the open," which "is none of the open's business" (44).

"Joseph Pockets" (*RC* 37–40) is a poem of the wanderer which defines pockets as vantage points from which we attempt to clarify and rectify both personal and cultural tragedy. It is one of many examples where Stern seems to set up verbal conditions which will compel him toward an "accidental" confrontation with the past or with issues of destiny. It begins in a typical nostalgic retrieval that creates an intersection between the Bible and the Great Depression:

> Have you ever lived through seven fat years and grown soft
> from eating lamb and bulgur? I remember lawyers
> standing in line for doughnuts and geniuses painting
> the walls of Idlewild Airport. . . .

Joseph, who was sold into slavery in Egypt to become a stranger and wanderer, enters the poem as a poetic mediator who "turns the past into a dream / and shows us how we lived and what disappeared." There are "Joseph pockets" in Pittsburgh, Detroit, or Chicago "where you can see / the dream turned around and the darkness illuminated, / some of the joy explained, some of the madness."

The speaker's quest leads him to a movie theater, presumably the one showing *The Hunger March,* a film about the Depression which he has described earlier in the poem.[6] He feels himself to be a stranger: "When I walked into the lobby I felt like a visitor." He finds a brief communion with the woman next to him, who touches him "on the little wooden arm" of his seat. The film is a Joseph pocket that illumines the past: "I lived in a Joseph pocket there. . . ."

Here I Am Walking

The poem goes on to describe the sights on a disturbing walk through Pittsburgh, its peregrinations pushing it restlessly on toward the unknown destination that compels it and which, in a sense, its *discursus* seeks to hold off: a mental visit to the Jewish cemetery in Carrick where Stern's sister and grandparents are buried, an arrival both dreaded and longed for.

When he first reaches the cemetery, the speaker feels "cut off," apparently from his tradition, since he has to borrow a prayer book:

> I borrow a book from the bleak office and open
> to the page to be read at the graveside of a sister.
> I ask her first to remember her shocking death
> and all the clumsiness and sadness of her leaving.
> I ask her to describe—as she remembers it—
> how I stood in front of her white coffin
> and stared at the mourners in our small living room.
> I ask her to think again about the two peach trees,
> how close together they were, how tiny their fruit was,
> forty years ago in the light rain,
> wherever she is, whatever sweet wing she's under.

This visit to the cemetery was gently prefigured by the visit to the movie theater, another "pocket" where the speaker felt estranged until a woman "touched" him. In other words, the movie theater scene is a minor realization of the poem's impulse, an attempt to mollify its dangerous currents which doesn't work; the poem pushes on toward a more overt enactment.

The speaker's entreaty to the sister is an attempt to soothe his unreasonable guilt; it is almost as if he asks her forgiveness. This particular past may never be fully accommodated; in a way, the Stern poem is always an effort to do so. But it is the "last Joseph pocket" for this poem. The speaker moves on, in imagination, to New York, "all the sorrows / of life disappearing . . . as we pick up speed going east on the empty turnpike."

"Arranging a Thorn" (L 32–33) is a tragi-comic poem in which the ancestral wandering poet is reborn on today's poetry circuit, the path of poets who wander from Hilton to Hyatt as they give readings. The hub is Newark Airport, where all roads meet:

> I am wandering through Newark, New Jersey,
> among the gymnasts, the accountants and the kings
> and my arms are breaking from all the weight I carry.

With his heavy briefcases and the other burden he carries, the speaker wanders endlessly "out of one long corridor and into another" and "through the beeper, over and over again, / discarding my metal, dropping my keys and watches." When he gets through the security check and onto the plane, he gets only "a slightly bored or slightly disdainful look" from the "drunken crew / and the food gatherers." He thinks of the low status of the poet: "I am ranked below the businessmen / with their two-suiters and their glasses of ice."

> —Ah brother Levine and brother Stanley Plumly,
> what hell we live in; we travel from Tuscaloosa
> to Houston; we go to Chicago; we meet the monster
> and spend our night at the Richmont or the Hyatt,

Stern's occasional apostrophes to other poets announce his membership in the brotherhood of poets from which he was long excluded. As reflections of the need for peer recognition, they represent the sibling aspect of his stance, which contrasts with the dominant and more mature father figure.

The bleak, comic travelogue continues to an anonymous hotel where "coffee and toast / is seven dollars," and to the reading itself, attended by only twenty people. The American bard is a sad reminder of his ancestor, having lost his audience, his usefulness: there is no call for a spiritual guide in a spiritless place. The old roaming poet was a binding influence who represented the values of the realm; the American bard is a stranger in his own land. The poem displays a grotesque dislocation between the poet's vocation and his practice; he is forced to collude in the sleazy, boring, airport world whose assumptions he doesn't share and to accept its prizes, which "are there for delusion." Poets have no choice but to "stand in the dust": "That's all there is."

Yet the poet has his private delight: "there is such joy in sitting here knowing / one thing from another; I feel like singing." Since he receives no hero's tribute from the culture, he crowns himself: "I make a garland for my head."[7] But it turns out to be a crown like that of the crucified prophet; he ends by "arranging a thorn."

The quest pattern seen in these poems of the wanderer is Stern's typical discovery procedure; it's a common pattern of the lyric, but extremely exaggerated. The opening identifies the point of departure; it tells you where the speaker is and what he's doing. The speaker moves out in an associative and discursive quest that leads to significance. The journey may take the questor into dangerous territory. The meaning he encounters may be painful. If so, he must wrest an affirmation from it; the poem must fulfill its tragic function.

It is convenient to speak of the wanderer and rabbi as separate characters in Stern, but they are clearly roles played by one encompassing character whose voice and gestures inhabit them both. They sometimes blur into one another, since the dichotomous positions they represent are viewed in shifting and ambivalent ways in the corpus. They merge not only with one another but also with other roles including plant and animal personae.

The wanderer's trope is the more overt and inherent, because it describes the procedure of the poem itself and matches Stern's inclinations: his sympathies tend to be anti-establishment. Yet he has never been able to accept the rejection of the past that goes with the revolutionary stance. The rabbi isn't named as frequently, but his function as an upholder of tradition is implicit throughout the canon. His role is confirming and consoling when compared with the often disturbing journey of the wanderer. As wise man, historian, teacher, and prophet of the tribe, he stands for an important aspect of the role of the poet.

I am calling this spiritual leader a rabbi, but in some cases he is a priest. The notable example is "Father Guzman," a book-length dramatic poem on the subject of love and politics. A dialogue between Father Guzman, a Maryknoll priest who is really a Jew from Brooklyn, and Boy, a Caribe Indian, the poem is much harsher and sharply ironic than Stern's other work. The priest is also the American ambassador and Christopher Columbus, two representations of the imperial agent. The boy is his servant, his pupil, and his alter ego. Boy takes various roles representing one who is oppressed, colonized, or acted upon; for instance, he becomes a dress, that is, a woman, who is victimized. Father Guzman and Boy both seek an Eldorado: the boy's is New York City, the priest's is justice. In the poem, the secret agenda is finally not politics but love.

Stern is a stranger and wanderer who sometimes wants to be a rabbi; under his nonconformist impulses is the wish to assume an official position, to be admitted to the canon. Even when his spokesman wanders in exile, he is drawn to the other side of the dualism: "When I drove through the little bald hills of Tennessee / I thought of the rabbis of Brooklyn bent over their psalms" (*LL* 58). He is uneasy, however, about the *profession* of rabbi, as he is about any profession, including that of the poet-professor. What he identifies with is the idea or myth of the rabbi as an ancient and venerable figure. The medieval rabbi, he says, upholds a tradition of virtue; the bourgeois rabbi of nineteenth- and twentieth-century America participates in a corrupt, materialistic vision.[8] The rabbi he idealizes is most like the Hassidic *zaddik*, literally a "righteous person," who was often, in fact, a wandering preacher. The *zaddikim* claimed their authority by virtue of their own righteousness and closeness to God rather than by official sanction. Their discursive, oral homilies were calculated, creative misreadings of the entire body of Jewish tradition. At the same time, they were deeply faithful to rabbinic law. Thus they are both violators and upholders of tradition—or representatives of an unorthodox tradition.

In "Burst of Wind between Broadway and the River" (*R* 48), the wanderer seeks the rabbinical side of himself, which he left behind in a dairy restaurant. We find him wandering "between the eighth and the seventh avenue." He goes "up thirty-eighth past Lerner and Bears / looking for the dairy restaurant in which my brain was stranded."

> There at the little chairs and the round tables
> the rebbes read and eat.
> I walk between them like a learned soul,
> nodding my head and smiling,
> doing the secret steps and making the signs,
> following the path of authority and silence,

He briefly pretends to the role of the rabbi, who follows "the path of authority." His secret steps and gestures can be seen as official practice, perhaps that of the worship service. But they sound Hassidic rather than Talmudic, suggesting an occult tradition outside regular channels. On the self-reflexive level, they refer us to the poet as *magos*.

"The Blink of an Eye" (*L* 50–51) is another poem where the wanderer wants to be a rabbi. But he isn't sure he remembers the words:

> I stretch my hand for silence
> before I put my fingers up to straddle
> the two orbs. If I can bend down I'll touch
> my forehead to some stone. If I can remember
> the music I will sing although the words
> may be a little shaky. What is the thought
> between two states? Which way should I turn? Deliver me,
> I say to the sun, deliver me, to the moon.

"I stretch my hand" describes a ritual motion common in Stern; the speaker raises his hand in a powerful gesture when he preaches. The statement suggests Isaiah, where "his hand is stretched out still" is a refrain. Stern's continual references to hands stem in part from biblical emphasis on the hand of God. He defines the import of hands in a poem devoted to the subject: "It is the hand that acts / for the spirit" (*L* 30).

The two orbs and the two states mentioned in "The Blink of an Eye" are sun and moon, day and night, life and death. They may hint also at Israel and Judah. And they imply two kinds of meaning, two kinds of deliverance: the daylight, conscious mode of established doctrine and the moonlight, unconscious mode of theosophy.

The poem continues as the speaker walks down the highway behind two calves in a pickup truck. In Stern, calves, like lambs, always suggest sacrificial animals rather than idols. The speaker has abandoned his car, which must have broken down. He decides that "this way / is best, walking behind the calves." He prepares his "story," in case he should be stopped by a state trooper or "in case / Rabbi Akiba should stop me or Rabbi Judah, / asking about night and the first three stars, / testing me on purification and prayer. . . ." Judah the Prince is compiler of the *Mishna*, a Talmudic source; Rabbi Akiba is the attributive author of the *Sepher Yetziruh*, a kabbalistic source. These two combine the official tradition of law, which is day, and the secret tradition of mystery, which is night.

In "Self Portrait" (*LL* 35–37), the speaker again imagines himself as rabbi. The poem begins at the window of the speaker's bathroom, where, as artist, he controls the scene by turning the light off and on. The trees outside remind him of Van Gogh as seen in the painter's series of self-portraits, and he's off on an extravagant, centrifugal tribute to the human spirit. In the first half of the poem, he identifies with Van Gogh as a wildly emotional, anti-establishment artist. The speaker too is a stranger, "sitting in Raubsville, / the only Jew on the river." He thinks of himself as a wanderer, "walking down my road," and of his meditative pockets, "my weeds and watery places / where I can go to rest between the scourges." Or rather, he thinks of himself thinking of himself, since all this is in the typical *I will* syntax. After a twenty-three-line sentence full of biblical repetitions, he breaks off and begins again: "—I will think of myself in my rabbi's suit."

Clearly, the rabbi's role isn't one the speaker always feels confident about. In "Burst of Wind," he isn't really a rabbi; he's doing a rabbi imitation. In "Blink of an Eye," he can't remember his part. And here, he only considers dressing up in a rabbi outfit.

"Self Portrait" continues as the speaker creates a utopian dream of "another artistic life" that is messianic and socialist. He enters a biblical litany of almost two pages which lists all those for whom he will dream it. It is for Van Gogh and for "all the lunatics of God." It widens to encompass the globe and the history of mankind, finally going back to "the first stones we dragged / out of the mountain," to "the Fire / out of which the burned doves flew looking for water," to an Edenic image of "the grass that clung to our slippery arms and legs," and all the way back to an early organism emerging from the water: "in memory of the nourishing sand in which we lay like dead fishes / slowly mastering the sky." The burned dove in this section is a good example of Stern's love of textual transgressions, even little ones; in this playful reversal of Noah's myth, the dove flies out of fire looking for water. The poem ends with tributes to Albert Einstein, Eugene Debs, and Emma Goldman. The messianic credo and the recitation of the tribe's story are two functions of tradition that Stern endorses without hesitation and displays constantly in his poem. They promote the rabbinical side of his dichotomy even when the speaker is not called rabbi.

The rabbi's role as teacher is most appealing to Stern. He sees the poet as a "teacher of sadness" (*PP* 20) whose vision transforms sorrow into regeneration. "Hidden Justice" (*PP* 16) is a lesson about revelation; in self-reflexive terms, the poem is itself the site where revelation occurs. The speaker imagines a tiny forest under a Christmas cactus where he will meditate:

Here I Am Walking

> This is where I'll go to breathe
> and live in darkness
> and sit like a frog, and sit like a salamander,
> and this is where I'll find a tiny light
> and have my vision
> and start my school—

This imaginary *topos* is, in one sense, the poem itself, the speaker's habitation as well as the stage where he delivers his message:

> I will put my small stage here
> under a thick leaf
> and I will eat and sleep and preach right here

His sermon is on justice, a central issue of the Bible, where to be just is to be right or righteous, to keep God's law, to uphold tradition: "I will live completely for the flowering, . . . my fingers clawing the air / looking for justice; / year after year the same, / my fingers clawing the air for hidden justice." Clawing the air is a gesture regularly used by Stern himself.[9]

The speaker preaches on justice again in "I Pity the Wind" (*PP* 52–53). He explains the workings of his poem, warning us that he speaks in metaphors, or riddles, and allusions:

> I am letting a broom stand
> for my speech on justice
> and an old thin handkerchief
> for the veil of melodrama I have worn for thirty years.
>
> I am dragging in Euripides
> for his strange prayer
> and my own true Hosea
> for his poem on love and loyalty.

Hosea is perhaps the finest of the biblical poet-prophets and a strong model for Stern. Tender, emotional, and deeply metaphorical, he writes in a wandering, illogical style, flowing and leaping from one subject to another. His prophecy is an extended metaphor that ends with an eloquent maxim on justice: "For the ways of the Lord are right, and the just shall walk in them."

After preaching, Stern's speaker turns to a meditative interlude that combines Zen-like practice with singing and ritual:

> I start my practice later,
> twenty minutes for breathing,
> twenty minutes for song,
> twenty minutes for liberation and ritual.

He ends with pity for himself: "I pity this hero, / so in love with fire, / so warlike, so bent on teaching."

"Tashlikh" (*L* 17–18) is a poem in which an ancient Jewish ceremony is reenacted on the banks of the Delaware, with the Stern speaker acting as rabbi. He describes the poem as if he were showing a picture in an album:

> This one shows me standing by the Delaware
> for the last time. There is a book in one hand
> and I am making cunning motions with the other,
> chopping and weaving motions to illustrate
> what I am reading, or I am just enlarging
> the text with my hand the way a good Jew did
> before the 1930's. . . .

Once again he "talks with his hands" as he explains the service, a ceremony observed at the start of Rosh Hashanah in which sins, represented by bits of bread, are cast into the water.

It's hard to imagine a word which calls up an aura of greater wisdom, dignity, and ancient authority than *rabbi*. Yet the rabbi's position as representative of the status quo doubles back on itself when we consider that the tradition he stands for has since biblical times been a stranger's tradition: as a Jew, the rabbi is also a wanderer. This dichotomous symbology is portrayed in "Berkeley" (*PP* 29), where the rabbi sojourns in the alien land of California.

> I am so blind and ignorant
> of West Coast flora. I saw the wood waver
> and the ground shake; I sat on my black briefcase
> looking up at the leaves. I who am so
> wondrous, I who always looked for Messiahs,
> I who gave opinions, caught up now
> in a new strangeness thousands of miles away

from my own cold river, learning quickly to eat
the other foods, learning to love
the way they do, walking after them
with my mouth half open, starting gently to teach,
doing the wind first, doing the dark old days
before there was even wind. . . .

He adapts quickly, learning to eat non-kosher food and to love California style. His kidding tone and tinge of self-mockery serve as usual to make self-inflation acceptable. He soon becomes a *targu-mānu* and starts to interpret primordial wisdom; as usual, he enacts or *does* it. His performance, which in fact was probably a reading or series of readings, ends, and he heads back to New York, "swinging my briefcase / with all the secrets inside. Keeping my secrets." Here again he suggests the mystical tradition, especially since he goes on to say he is thinking about Poland, seat of Hassidism.

There's a sense in which the rabbi contains the dualism between the native and the stranger in one figure. He expresses the urge to resolve the restless dialogue between stasis and disruption. Neither of these tendencies, alone, is an appropriate guide; they are complementary.

The particular rabbi who for Stern most fully expresses the union of tradition and revolution is Jesus. As body and spirit, sufferer and transformer, he is a figure for Stern's ideal of the poet. In this Stern claims Emerson as a source. He notes that in *Nature*, Emerson spoke specifically of "the need for an intermediary or archangel who would be to the nation what Christ was to the first Christians. . . . The poet, acting from his own character, acts for us all. He is the representative man. He is Christ. Homer" ("What Is This Poet?" 153).

Stern's ideal is summed up in the emblem of a man both representative and Orphic, Homeric and Christlike, an adherent and a revolutionary. He doesn't apologize for the familiar, romantic eloquence of his stance. Instead, he regrets the fact that poets "seem to have chosen a less dramatic, shall I say less Orphic, view of themselves": "they have lost the great memory" ("What Is This Poet?" 155).

Jesus is an appropriate model for Stern's hero in several ways. Most obviously, he is a symbol of transformation. He is a metaphor for the idea that we have a spiritual destiny beyond, yet not distinct from, our creaturely life. He is also a rabbi who becomes a rebel, who exiles himself from the academy to become a stranger, then returns from his testing ground as prophet and even as God, establishing a new tradition rooted in the old. He is a radical who proves the very tradition he wants to revise, since he is a fulfillment of prophecy. He unites the Old Testament, seat of fear and prophecy, with the New Testament, seat of pity and fulfillment, to embody the tragic vision. His performance on the cross is a portrayal of divine sorrow, which we can only imagine in terms of God's death.

Stern's concept of Jesus is reconstituted, as are other traditional symbols that he adopts. He repudiates the Christian imagery of a meek, ethereal figure: he has "contempt for the lamb." And he rejects the concept of self-sacrifice, a Christian, not a Jewish, idea. Stern's Jesus is "a gnomic, a Zen master. He's elusive. He's angry and loving. He's violent." Stern also refuses the term *Christ*, because it is not a name but an originally Greek word signifying one who is anointed, sanctified or consecrated. Even the comparatively neutral name *Jesus* has accumulated an array of implications, including its use as a profanity. Stern uses *Jesus* in the poems for clarity, but he prefers *Joshua* or the Hebrew *Yehōshūa*, Jesus's original name. Because it takes the figure back to its origins, it allows a fresh interpretation. Reviving the Jewish origins of Jesus allows Stern entry, as a Jew, into the brotherhood of this significant person.[10]

Hints of Jesus appear now and then in the Stern speaker's protean performance. He says, "I guess you should weep for me" (*R* 39). He wears a crown of thorns (*L* 33). He counts the days till Easter, realizing that "noone will see me dying there in the twilight, / holding my hands up in the slippery branches" (*PP* 54). He says "there is a life to come," "I want the chance to live again"—or rather, a Mexican mosquito says this, speaking for the colonized. The speaker, a colonizer, kills the mosquito and then, like Jesus, has blood on his palms (*PP* 63).

"Stolen Face" (*L* 77–81) is a long, roving consideration of the transgressive nature of art which centers in the image of Christ. The speaker wanders the Piazza St. Andreas, in Lucca, Italy. He studies the religious statuary of a medieval stone arch, closing on a particular head that catches his attention. He notes that art goes beyond representation to incarnation: "one line / crossing another line, just that, and the flesh / is suddenly there." The idea of incarnation leads to a consideration of Jesus as an art object. As a spiritual idea represented in flesh, he is, in his person, a work of art. Beyond that, he has been continually recreated in painting. The speaker remembers a book "showing the faces of Jesus for five hundred years." Jesus is a "stolen face," usurped in a variety of Christian interpretations which deny his original Jewish identity. The speaker illustrates this by listing a number of paintings from different times and places, a Botticelli, a Juan Juarez, a Van Eyck, and others. One face is "thin and care-worn," another is "broken with pain," still others are "full of self-pity," "matter of fact," or "thoughtful."

The speaker soon begins to consider his own face; he "steals" it by converting it to an art object: "I put / the lines in the cheek—I think I like them wavy." As a figure in an artwork, or the speaker of a poem, he can invent himself as he chooses. He can make himself universal:

> I am the one from Asbury Park, I am
> the one from New Orleans, the one from France,
> the one from Philadelphia. I believe
> the Jews of Russia came from Asia, but the Jews
> of Poland came from Spain and Africa.

The significant words here are *I am the one*: the speaker tentatively puts himself forward as the poet-hero.

At this point the poem swerves into an obscure, half-hidden response to the relationship between Jew and Christian, an issue implicit in the confrontation of the speaker, a Jew, with Christian art. The speaker observes the man in the moon, another version of the stolen face, which now becomes a representative of medieval Christianity—as are the statues in the Piazza St. Andreas, where the speaker is an alien. He metamorphoses, becoming a medieval Jew who must show his credentials, things that prove he's a Jew, his "sack of old clothes," his "permits to trade with the East," his "bills of lading."[11] As the poem ends, the stolen face preaches a sermon, meant to represent the conversion sermons Jews were forced to attend in the Middle Ages.[12] It elicits an ironic, tongue-in-cheek response from the speaker: "I will convert, believe me." The point is that he will not convert, that his admiration for Jesus is not a flirtation with Christianity but wholly that of a fellow Jew. He asserts his right to "steal back" the figure of Jesus for his own art.

Stern's mythopoeic mind, enchanted by amalgamation and transformation, does not always see the Jewish and Christian traditions as mutually exclusive; they are sometimes aspects of one myth that is itself but a manifestation of archetypal patterns.

"Sycamore" (*PP* 59–61) is an intoxicating enactment of mythic intertextuality. A dazzle of transformation, full of gods and goddesses, song and dance, it rushes out in so many directions that it would fly apart were it not reined in by the voice of the speaker. Stern has given a detailed gloss of this poem that illustrates his persuasions. He even glosses his gloss, explaining his comments on the poem:

> I am treating the poem on its own terms, though in the real world, wherever that is, the world of good logic and reasonable transition and sanity, what happens (in the poem) is a little outrageous. The humor and tension consist in accepting, without too much question, the outrage. ("'Sycamore': Poem and Commentary" 9)

The poem begins in quiet celebration of a particular tree, seen just before spring, with last year's dead leaves "hanging in the wind like little hearts." The tree soon becomes a "twenty-arm goddess"; she teases the lord of lords, who is not only Christ but any idea of God. In his commentary, Stern points out that she is

> a kind of Shiva, that murderous goddess, but she is, at most, playful, making outrageous and vulgar gestures to the lord of lords, whoever he is, Apollo, God, The Force, Reality, her dance partner. (7)

In what Stern calls a "formal preparation for spring," the speaker takes the winter coverings off the windows, admitting cleansing light. A little wind enters, which the poet says is an allusion to Vana, the first god. The globalizing gesture of the poem continues as the speaker briefly becomes Old Shivers, a character Stern identifies as a "playful male counterpart of Shiva" (7–8). He does a spring dance: "a turn to the left, to the right."

Turning again to the tree, the speaker thinks of its snakelike habit of shedding its bark, or skin, each year, in habitual rebirth. This leads to a consideration of reincarnation which Stern glosses in his commentary:

> I take up the religious celebration of rebirth, . . . called
> "Passover" in the Jewish faith, as it is called "Easter" in the
> Christian, and I emphasize liberation, freedom, the life to
> come, Easter and Passover things, albeit with a little irony, . . .
> outrageously selecting de Leon's (and the middle class's) Flor-
> ida as the promised land. (8)

The next figures in the poem are Daphne and Apollo. Stern notes
that Daphne represents the rejection of spring and rebirth, Apollo
its violent affirmation (8). In a glittering display of *tekhnē*, the
speaker enacts a series of quick transformations wrapped in a skein
of verbal strategy and untrackable syntax. The tree becomes Apollo;
the speaker becomes Daphne, who enters the tree to live for a year
until rebirth. Then the speaker shifts roles to become the tree—or
he will, he could, he might. He might "do some flashy / two-step
that's made for sycamores," a dance step much like the pattern of
this poem.

In the long, final passage, the speaker looks forward to a Seder
where he will officiate as rabbi. Stern's discussion of this section
clarifies his view of the Old and New Testaments as modulations of
old, engulfing myth:

> Passover is a holiday which celebrates freedom and condemns
> slavery and uses the Jewish experience as a primary exem-
> plification. It is, to compare it to Easter, as if the liberation of
> the Jewish people from their slavery in Egypt was exactly the
> same as the liberation of the spirit from its earthly body. Of
> course, that liberation precedes, and goes beyond, both of these
> religions. (9)

Stern goes on to note that "the cultish spring festival, with all its
pastoral and agricultural roots, has been historicized and preempted
by the Exodus celebration." (9)

> Moreover, this particular ritual meal and the primitive original,
> and all the myths and rites alluded to are references to some-
> thing much deeper in the human psyche; they are all ropes
> thrown into the dark water and that is the reason, probably, for
> both the humor and the sadness. (10)

The Seder section begins, Stern tells us, at the point in the meal where the leader elaborates on the meaning of the holiday (9). Though Stern does not comment on the self-reflexive level of the poem, it is clear that the speaker's remarks have to do not only with Passover but also with the poem itself. He plans to offer a lesson on the tree; he will ask: "How does it serve as a text / for lives that are pinched, or terrified?" On one level, this "it" is the poem. He will "go on for an hour storming and raving"—as he does in the poem. He asks to be forgiven for turning into a tree, and in a typically inclusive, comic gesture, he even offers a Jewish apology to the Egyptians for "leaving you suddenly."

The poem is filled with both affirmation and doubt; these tensions are not fully resolved, as the poet explains:

> I end as I began, with a complicated and ambiguous attitude to the tree and to existence itself, though I suspect that, on a psychological level, there is a kind of final affirmation after the internal struggle between the forces of life and death, realized as mixtures of pain and pleasure, and that is what both the confusion and the urgency are about. (10)

In the final lines, the speaker embodies a synthesis between rabbi and wanderer, tradition and transformation. He is the spiritual leader who enacts familiar ritual: he is in charge of "the service," since he's "the only one in this house." Both the service and the house can be taken literally and also as the poem itself, which he rules. At the same time, he is a rebel who acts for himself alone and does as he pleases. He becomes a metaphor for transformation, a "flowering figure" of vast proportions who takes dangerous chances or "leans far out" in the course of his wanderings.

> I'll end
> by sprinkling the tree and sprinkling the ground around it
> and holding my hand up for a second of silence,
> since I am the one who runs the service—I am
> the only one in this house, I do my reclining
> all alone, I howl when I want, and I am,
> should anyone come in, a crooked tree
> leaning far out, I am a hundred feet tall,
> I am a flowering figure, I am staggering
> across the desert, and here I am now in New York
> and here I am now in Pittsburgh, the perfect wilderness.

⇒ V ⇐

Flying without a Shadow

At the apex of Stern's baroque statuary stands the emblem of an angel whose capacity for flight is grounded by the gardener at its base. The undertext of figurative relationships in the corpus as a whole is felt as a containing and organizing presence behind its local discursiveness: nostalgia conveys us to the garden, which points to the expulsion and the *figūra* of the wanderer, which plays against its companion figure, the rabbi. Overlooking all these is the angel, source of inspiration and transformation. These spokesmen and their plots entwine endlessly, like the voices of a musical canon, discouraging progression in favor of an atmosphere of recurrence, even simultaneity.

In the angel, Stern takes on his most familiar and therefore most challenging figure. Its symbology brings a heavier baggage than almost any personage one could undertake to reinvent, from popular lore, painting, and the poets. From Roethke's angel, a "field of light"; to Rilke's, which transmutes the visible into the invisible; to Stevens's "necessary angel of earth"; to Shelley's "lost angel of a ruined Paradise"; to Blake's dark guide—the poetic appeal of angels goes on back through Milton and Dante to the Bible itself and beyond, into the old, polytheistic gods and spirits who are the progenitors of angels.

Mal'ach, the Hebrew word for *angel*, does not in itself imply divinity. It originally referred to a messenger or agent who performs a *melachah*, an ordinary human mission.[1] In the early part of the Bible narrative, the characters we know as angels were originally men, evil spirits, or minor gods. The term *mal'ach* was substituted later, partly in an effort to suppress remnants of polytheism.[2] For instance, in the original Genesis, Jacob didn't wrestle with an angel but with an evil spirit in the form of a man. Hosea, in the mid-eighth century B.C., was the first to comment on this ancient Israelite legend using the term *mal'ach*. The winged beings we typically imagine stem from the seraphim, or "flaming ones," seen in Isaiah; they reflect Babylonian influence and are the first manifestation in the Bible of a definite concept of angels.

Angels don't begin to play a role in Jewish theology until the post-Exilic period, when the prophet Zechariah envisions Gabriel, the messenger angel, Ezekiel the scribe, and other angelic creatures including two females. Two well-known angels, Michael and Gabriel, are among the many who appear in the book of Daniel. These angels have human weaknesses; Gabriel, for instance, is subject to physical weariness. Jewish angelology develops intricately in subsequent apocalyptic and Talmudic writings. In the latter, angels number in the billions; each Jew is accompanied by as many as eleven thousand angels. But the elaboration of complicated systems of angels reaches its peak in the kabbala; during the period of popular, debased kabbalism, magical practices caused the Jews to be labeled angel worshippers.

It is against this Old Testament background, not primarily as a reaction to the poets, that Stern's idea of the angel coheres; among poets' angels, his is the only one of Jewish descent. No doubt, the figure appeals to him because it contains many characters, as does his speaker. The primordial origins of the figure please him, as does its human nature, seen in early Bible stories. And he appreciates its long standing as a potent symbol. He is unconsciously drawn to the challenge of *réchauffé*; the more debilitated an image, the more inventive he becomes. His tendency is always to go back to the origins of a trope and start over; far beneath the debilitated, Christmas card outlines of our vestigial angel, he discovers weight and substance.

There has never been an angel anything like Stern's raffish stand-in. Needless to say, he's the same tragi-comic vagabond we have come to know in other guises. A nonidealized, humanistic angel, he stands for the spirit of the intermediary, the poet carrying a message about life and death. He is also an incarnation of the dream of change: like man, he is spirit locked in flesh, but he can move freely in time and space and transform himself endlessly without disappearing. Thus, he is imagination stained with blood and suffering. He embodies the ultimate nostalgic impulse, since he is a partly human person whose memory is eternal. In all this, he is not only one of the forms of the Stern speaker but the key to them all.

The angel plays a leading part in only a few poems. In "The Expulsion," which I have already examined, the angel of death is not an aspect of the speaker but another character, an "angry mother." She does, however, share some of the symbolism of the speaker-angel; she is art and imagination.[3] The meanings of the angel are omnipresent in the corpus; they come to a head and cohere as a role of the speaker in several poems from *The Red Coal*.

"The Angel Poem" (*RC* 45–49), a five-page fable, is the primary enunciation of the figure. I want to treat it in close detail, as a central and definitive poem in the Stern canon. One of its charms is the brilliant shift in which the angel imagines humans, rather than the reverse. He is like the dog, in the poem of that name, who depicts man, his master.[4] In both cases, the reversal subverts sentiment and provides the opportunities of a fresh perspective.

In the first three stanzas of "The Angel Poem," the angel-speaker introduces and describes himself. In so doing, he takes up two related subjects: the fragility of life, and pain, which is the angel's human portion. His first words announce that he is flawed, disfigured, fallen:

> My broken wing is on the left near the large joint
> that separates me so crazily from half the others.
> I think of trees and how they break apart
> in the wind, how sometimes a huge branch
> will hang in strips, what would be skin
> in humans or angels, and how the flesh
> Is like pulp, and almost blood-red where the break is.

Because the broken wing is on the left, it awakens the imagery of left-handedness—and its opposition with right-handedness—significant throughout Stern. In another poem, the speaker imagines his left hand as "consisting of four feminine angels / and one crooked broken masculine one" (*RC* 68). In still another, as he dreams of light returning at dawn, he imagines that his hand is reborn: "my five dry fingers / returning to life" (*L* 24). Even a trivial thing like a numb hand in sleep has, for Stern, transcendent implications.

The phrase "half the others," seen above in the opening of "The Angel Poem," is one of those collapsed, disruptive Sternian references that resists interpretation. Does it refer to females, half the human race? If so, it's part of a confused sexual joke with the male "large joint" out of place. "The others" recurs later in the poem, where it refers to other poets. The phrase appears in other poems as well; in "Clay Dog" (*PP* 8) it seems to refer to other art objects. In general, the phrase suggests common humanity.

The tree metaphor of this opening passage enters into Stern's complex imagery of the tree, for which "Sycamore" is the key poem. Here, it serves to place the angel in nature: the wheeling syntax of the *how* clauses draws the angel into the picture of the tree. The last clause of the section can refer to the tree or to "humans or angels"; the wounded speaker, like the tree, has flesh and—almost—blood. This illustrates how Stern uses anaphora to display the spirit of transformation in syntax. The metaphor is crucial: when the angel is seen as a part of nature, the imagination is placed there also.

The speaker goes on to explain the pain in his wing, which reminds him of shoulder pain, that is, human pain. Our response to him is one of sympathy, even empathy, a reaction quite different from the awe and distance we feel in the presence of most angels.

> I tend to drag the wing because the pain
> in lifting it is too much for me to stand.
> That part of me that is still human recalls
> what pain in the shoulder can be, and I remember
> not only the sharp stabs when I had to turn
> but the stiffness that made me keep my arm at my side
> and forced me to plan my eating and my sad sleeping.

The wing is spirit; the dragged burden of spiritual pain is made comprehensible by comparing it with physical hurt. The source of *pain* in the Greek *poinē*, or *penalty*, reminds us that fallen angels were penalized for consorting with humans. In some accounts, angels are creatures deprived of paradise, as man was in the expulsion, when he first suffered. In Stern's reversal, the angel was once fully human. If the angel is the poet, then the poet, in his imaginative flight, is charged to remember human pain.

In the next trope, the angel-speaker further identifies himself in a bird metaphor. The many birds in Stern are one of the ways the angel's signal is carried over into other material; besides the natural affinities between birds and angels, there are intimations of angels in some of Stern's bird images that lead us to see angelic echoes in them all. In one poem there are "six birds sitting like little angels / in the white birch tree" (PP 39). In another, the speaker becomes an angelic songbird-poet: "I'm folding my wings in front of my chest / and rubbing my beak through the inner feathers," "reaching notes beyond my hearing or caring" (PP 38). In still another, some swans "dream of spreading their terrifying wings"; they wish they could be flying horses with "drops of mercy pouring from their eyes, / bolts of wisdom from their foreheads" (RC 3). These horses imagined by the swans remind me of the red ones that used to appear on Mobil signs, which stem from winged mythological creatures, including angels like the winged horses in Zechariah. Here, their mercy and wisdom suggest that they're angels or old gods.

The winged intermediaries of "These Birds" (RC 78) are surely angels. They "bring their bodies with them" and act "as if they could drink and eat with impunity": haggadic interpreters sometimes note that angels can't eat mortal food. The birds act "as if their wings gave them the right to stand there"; "as if there were not another life to think of"; "as if they had not already created the first darkness." In "June First" (RC 32), the angel's trope is even conveyed into the image of seed pods that "spin in the wind": we "pick / them up gingerly to see if they had wings" and "break them open to see what made them fall."

The bird chosen in "The Angel Poem" is the anti-romantic, anti-heroic pigeon, a homely member of the dove family. It appears again in a later poem with its "left claw bent," recalling the broken left wing of the angel-pigeon we see here. Here it is contrasted with the hawk, a militaristic hero. It quickly loses its humility as the speaker goes on to describe it in a gaudy image:

> As far as birds, I am more like a pigeon than a hawk.
> I think I am one of those snow-white pigeons with gold
> eyes and a candy-corn beak, with a ruffled
> neck—a huge white hood—and ruffled
> legs, like flowers or long white pantaloons,

This swanky image illustrates how Stern uproots a traditional figure like the angel by moving it out into a variety of metaphors. The bright, idealized pigeon quickly modulates back into a realistic one who is frightened, falls on some "dirty newspapers," and flies "with shame"; his fall and his shame are a glance at fallen angels as well as the eviction. He rises "with effort"; after his fall, laden with humanity, he barely remembers how to fly. The pigeon imagery of this poem, which combines a humble street character and a showy bird, is one of the best descriptions the Stern speaker gives us of himself.

After these introductory stanzas, the theme of the poem is directly stated as the imagery of rising, flying, and falling continues:

> My main thought is how I can translate pain
> into a form that I can understand,
> so I break a wing or bruise my foot; but the wound
> is more like panic, more like flying
> without a shadow or flying in darkness,
> something like the human dream when fear
> makes them rise out of a sound sleep
> and move without control above their bodies,
> along the ceiling or through the closed windows,
> pushing and yelling as they fall through the glass.

Rising and falling is the spatial pattern of recurring rebirth and death which contrasts throughout Stern with bipolar, left-right alternation. The imagined out-of-body flight in these lines is a negative version of the spontaneous rising seen in some of Stern's epiphanies. Afterward, both the angel and the human he has imagined "have bloody feathers."

In the next stanza, the speaker reports that he has studied the history of angels: "I have looked myself up in the Jefferson Market Library. . . ." Probably, after the angel appeared in the course of his work, Stern did look up the early biblical, haggadic, and kabbalistic sources of the figure. These come into the poem as the speaker describes his study of "winged servants" and the angel hierarchies of "the Moors and the Akkadians." He decides he must be "one of the million / Enoch encountered on his first trip to Heaven."

The distinction between Stern's speaker and himself is almost too obvious to point out in a device such as this. In the poem, Gerald Stern doesn't go to the library; the angel goes to look himself up. This difference is clearly critical. It transforms what could be boring exposition about angels into characterization, as the angel seeks his heritage. He incorporates into himself the history of angels:

> I know I am also the dark part of the leaf,
> that I walk upright, that I am half snow, half fire,
> that I can move like light from one end of the house to
>   the other,
> that I have something in common with Tammuz, and with
>   Shelley.

The phrase "half snow, half fire" suggests a haggadic interpretation wherein angels consist of a compatible combination of fire and water. Tammuz, the tenth month in the Hebrew calendar, is derived from the Babylonian *Du'uzu*, a god whose name means "the son who rises." Thus, the speaker-angel-bird, who rises clumsily, has "something in common" with Jesus. In joining an ancient Babylonian god with Shelley, Stern points to the long and universal background of the angel figure.

The next passage is a long, vivid, idiosyncratic, and richly allusive commentary on the angel-speaker's visit to the Jefferson Market Library. Like a good angel, he helps the humans he meets there. This passage ends as the speaker pauses and drops his voice. He turns again to the subject of suffering:

> All those who live in pain go on fixed walks
> between two stations and mark the passage with drops
> of blood. They push against each other, bruising
> their delicate shoulders and legs—who would know
> that one man's stomach is gone, that one has ankles
> the size of balloons, that one is in terror
> of impotence, that one has blood in her throat.

The sudden directness of this moving passage gains importance through its immersion in the fabular tapestry of the poem. The stations between which man struggles back and forth are major intersections or subway stations and also the stations of the cross. The hissing phrase "fixed walks" exemplifies the skillful use of sound which we could afford to linger over in a minimal poem. In the next passage of the poem, these rigid, inescapable paths are contrasted with the fluid escapades of Stern's familiar wanderer.

The angel-speaker merges with the figure of the wanderer and begins an excursion that takes him from Twelfth Street and Sixth Avenue to Fourteenth Street, past the Greenwich Savings Bank and Corby's Bar and past a dead pigeon who was, earlier in the poem, himself, stumbling and falling on the sidewalk. He pays tribute to the Vitamin Quota; to the former Wanamaker's department store, a "kind of Parthenon" which is now "lost"; and the aptly named Paradise Cafeteria, which is, aptly, empty. As always, the factual accuracy of the terrain stabilizes Stern's fanciful ramblings.

At Eighth Avenue, the speaker is joined by "the others": "we make our way down our own Dolorosa / like chirping grasshoppers and gurgling pigeons." These others might be Dreiser, Dostoevsky, and Balzac, observers of human suffering who were seen earlier in the poem with "wings over their leather coats." They suggest all poets, since when they reach the Port Authority, they are represented as music makers. Music, or poetry, is illegal there, "so we put down our combs and potatoes / and walk away—like the others— with crushed vision." The speaker hopes they can all go together to the seashore, where they can sing "with no constraints."

In a common Stern pattern, the poem shifts to future tense and hooks back to its opening image in preparation for consummation: "I think the sea and the sea air will mend / my stiff arm." The hurt wing becomes an arm; the speaker resumes his life as a man. He plans to lie in the water "humming my new poems." In an egocentric fantasy, he imagines that he will become a giant when other poets have faded: "I know that when the others / go, like mist, or gray jelly, or tiny crabs / I will lie on the sand and make my own imprint." It will be huge, "seven or eight feet this time, a giant / sand angel."[5] He will make this image not with a broken stick, as in the early "Rejoicings," but as humans make snow angels, by moving his arms.

The image will be discovered by two children who "run up to the iron benches / shouting":

> "An angel, an angel, there was an angel lying
> on our beach; he was ten feet tall and his wings
> were curved at the top like the white bird at school.
> We saw him fly over the old Imperial,

> then bounce on top of the huge red tiles
> and bow—like a drunk—to the dancing whale,"[6]

Needless to say, this clownish angel is the speaker, who often bows to his audience. He will watch the children discover him. Then he will leave the poem: he will "walk down to the yellow bus station" and buy a ticket for "Easton, Pennsylvania, or New York, New York."

The image discovered by the children is a parallel for "The Angel Poem" itself. The movement of the poem as a whole leads from the subject of pain to the children's moment of delight and belief, dramatizing Stern's traditional faith in the power of imaginative transformation to bring beauty out of suffering.

"Lord, Forgive a Spirit" (*RC* 16–17), is a lighter, more playful treatise on the angel which connects him to the garden trope. He appears as a muse or messenger who inspirits the speaker, distinct from, yet an aspect of himself. Like the speaker, he is a poet and also a gardener. He appears in a backyard Eden equipped with a ladder which suggests the one used by angels to get back and forth from heaven to earth (Genesis 28: 12).[7]

> So what shall we do about this angel,
> growing dizzy every time he climbs a ladder,
> crying over his old poems.
> I walk out into the garden and there he is,
> watering the lilies and studying the digitalis.
> He is talking to his own invisible heart;
> he is leaking blood.

Fear of heights is a serious problem for an angel, but this one has a more profound human weakness: trouble with his heart. He studies digitalis, a cardiac stimulant. Like the protagonist of "The Angel Poem," he spills human blood. He is partly a heroic art image, like a statue shining in the sun: "His eyes flash with fire, his eyelashes blaze and / his skin shines like brass, / but he trips in the dirt just like any gardener, or grieving poet." Like the speaker, he is a nexus of art and everyday life.

In his presence the poet-speaker is inspired: "I sit in the sun and fill a whole new book / with scrawls and symbols." In this poem, the angel bespeaks art and the lost past, "gold leaf / and the half-forgotten ruins."

117

> he tries to remember his old words—
> his old songs, his first human songs—
> lost somewhere in the broken glass and the cinders,
> a foot below the soft nails and the hinges.

Here the angel assumes a pivotal role as the agent of a profound nostalgia which seeks reunion with origins.

In "Rotten Angel" (*RC* 5–6), the speaker describes his own funeral. Here again, a twist of perspective defamiliarizes a potentially sentimental scene. The burial site is a half-submerged island just south of Stern's home on the river in Raubsville, Pennsylvania.[8] The speaker's friends go with him "to the bottom of the river." They are "drinking beer and crying" as he waits for "the rotten angel," Malachamovitz, who visits a Jew when he dies.[9] This river and island appear again and again in the corpus; they play into old river myths where the god's death signifies renewal. In one poem, the speaker explains their significance: "Oh Babylonian, I am swimming in the deep off the island / of my own death and birth" (*RC* 57). This Babylonian could be an angel, since the first Jewish depiction of angelic figures was borrowed from Babylonia.[10]

The "rotten angel" plays only a minor part in this poem. He never actually appears and is mentioned only twice. At the start, he is an awaited presence, expected not only by the dead speaker but also by the reader. At the end, he has already been there; the speaker imagines "how the angel must have gasped as he swam / back to the shore. . . ." The only thing we know about him is the human weakness seen in his gasping. He is what we're waiting for and what has passed unseen.

The body of the poem does not deal explicitly with the angel but with the speaker. Though dead, he reaches his arms up into the branches, then falls down, worn out from "fighting for air," as the angel will be later in the poem; this shared imagery blurs the distinction between man and angel: both crave the breath of life. After describing the scene, the "sad ritual," and even the "iron bird" he plans to have on his grave, the speaker suddenly steps outside the scene, admitting that it's an invention. In a major tone shift accompanied by the usual dash, he says: "—How I would love it if I could really be buried here. . . ." The word *really* is strong in this context; the speaker seems to have made a rare disappearance, leaving the poet himself exposed. He goes on to express his wish to "be connected / with life as long as possible," to "disappear slowly, . . . so there is time / for those who want to see me in my own light / and get an idea of how I made my connections / and what I looked at and dreamed about. . . ." Here the poet reveals his fear of disappearing and hope for the survival of his art. Stern often affirms the possibility that redemption has to do not with being saved but with saving everything: "my mind / goes back, it is a kind of purse, nothing / is ever lost" (L 67). The closing of "Rotten Angel" winds out into a litany of remembrance that fastens the speaker to the gasping angel, his invention, his spirit, almost himself.

The dramatic potential of "Rotten Angel" is incompletely realized. Minor in itself, it gains through participation in the intricate network of cross-references that synchronize the corpus. Recurring variations on the same archetypal dramas and insistent repetition of the same metaphors complicate and enrich the text and inspire a quality of simultaneity. The dramatic idea of "Rotten Angel" is collapsed into one line of "Picking the Roses," where the speaker imagines himself as "a ghost at my own funeral" (PP 6). In another of the many poems which refer to the same story, the speaker again insists on the ghost figure, a close relative of the angel: "It was my ghost, my old exhausted ghost, / that I dressed in white, and sent across the river, / weeping and weeping and weeping / inside his torn sheet" (LL 28). The trip to the river is one of a number of plots in Stern that gains the status of ritual through reenactment.

The breath metaphor of "Rotten Angel" also appears often in the canon. The speaker seems to look back on this poem when he says in a later one, "I was gasping then, / trying to get a breath, and I am gasping / now, my rib is broken, or bruised . . ." (L 67). At one point, the speaker remembers "floating into the weeds" and "lying on the coarse sand reaching up for air" (RC 34). In another place, he considers "the last breath left / after a lifetime of tearful singing" (PP 3). At still another, he imagines "how foolish the body / must feel when it's only a carcass, when the breath / has left it forever" (PP 61).

In particular, the water burial and related imagery of falling and rising seen in "Rotten Angel" are archetypes omnipresent in Stern; often they lead to rebirth. The speaker is always "trying to rise" in "the wet leaves and the grass and the flowers . . . and the weeds and the water" (RC 22).

"The Sensitive Knife" (*LL* 21) is a version of the river story which leads to rebirth through the Passover ritual. The speaker is seen "walking the towpath," "climbing the stone island," and "swimming the river." He both sits and kneels, typically combining Hassidic and Zen practice with the vocabulary of traditional prayer. He soon transforms himself into a huge bird or angel with "two-foot wings" that moves through the branches of black locusts, Stern's "Jewish tree." Man, angel-bird, and tree merge as he imagines himself coming apart: "I think of my own legs as breaking off / or my wings coming loose in the wind / or my blossoms dropping onto the ground." Here he seems to lose all his assumptions about form or identity, becoming a part of nature's inevitable falling away. But at once he notices signs of rebirth: "Across the river the sticks are coming to life / and Mithras and Moses and Jesus are swaying and bowing / in all directions." Here he imagines the moving trees as holy figures, signs of renewed faith. He swims "carefully through the blood" and sees his father laying out "the shank bone / and the roasted egg on a white napkin." The spring celebration of rebirth is also a reunion with the past: "I climb over the rhododendrons and the dead trees to meet him."

Another variation on the river myth is seen in "One Foot in the River" (*LL* 5). It displays the deathly passage downward without the upward movement of rebirth. The speaker goes to the bottom of the water where he can "live for days in a cold state / beside the catfish and the bony shad." He sees "a butchered face" go by in the water and watches "the blood come." Reminders of mortality, of suffering, appear even in this deathly state.

"Leaving Another Kingdom" (*PP* 23–24) dramatizes another excursion to the burial site, this time with Stern's friend the poet Philip Levine. The ritual journey, always a potentially hazardous one, becomes an enactment of the poet's ability—and indeed his continual inclination—to reimagine the past and combine it with ordinary life in a constantly developing myth. The poet-speaker plans that he and his companion will "walk the mile to my graveyard . . . going over the past a little, / changing a thing or two, / making a few connections. . . ." He imagines them "walking down to the end of the island / so we could put our feet in the water. . . ." The real-life hike, itself imagined, becomes a heady romance as the poem wheels into a forty-nine-line gerund modifying the word *poets*. The river mutates into the "dangerous channel" where

"Tristan / and his Isolt, Troilus and you know who, / came roaring by" on inner tubes. As the huge sentence ends, it finds the two poets entering the water in a heightened image that sounds almost baptismal: "walking into the water, / leaving another island, leaving another / retreat, leaving another kingdom." They seem to leave this life, which is an island, for another.

In "For Song" (PP 27), the crucial river setting is a *topos* for the contemplation of paradise. The speaker begins "thirty feet above the water" but soon descends to find his "place in the scheme of things" among the tribes of Israel, between the nations of Reuben and Dan. He is considering the divine plan, "paying attention to providence," which is revealed by silver fishes who are also angels, "the silver hordes this time." In mud to his knees, he is "studying paradise and the hereafter, / a life beyond compare." He finds it in nature, a "blade of grass," "a dozen fruits and flowers," a recovered Eden that instigates his music. He claps "for harmony" and listens "to the worms / for song."

This traditional and rather simplistic kind of inspiration through nature sometimes occurs in Stern's short poem. More often, especially in longer poems, it is complicated or undermined by various kinds of designification. The Stern speaker also turns occasionally to painting and often to music for inspiration or salvation: "listening to Bach and resurrecting my life" (PP 34). He is touched by Yehudi Menuhin, Jascha Heifitz, and "the great Stern himself / dragging his heart from one ruined soul to another" (PP 11). By referring to Isaac Stern without mentioning the first name, he engages in a bit of teasing self-puffery.

Underlying all the sources of transcendence displayed in the corpus is the tragic potential of sorrow and suffering. In "Steve Dunn's Spider" (PP 10), a more complex and satisfying version of the pattern seen in "For Song," a comic river quest leads to the issue of suffering. The word *down* is repeated six times as the speaker descends through "sweet pepper bushes," to a "nudist's log" in the water, to "the fat girl's tried and true paradise."[11] He says he will avoid reminders of suffering "at any cost" but goes on at once to mention several, including "the oozing ankle," and "the year of remorse"; the subject is unavoidable. The poem demonstrates the risk inherent in transformation: heaven suddenly becomes hell, the "twenty-fourth or twenty-fifth circle" of an enlarged Dantean inferno. The river swimming hole where the poem began has become "a pool of warm blood." The speaker tries to save himself by holding onto a tree, as he does in "Rotten Angel," but finally goes "to the furthest limit." He descends by "free will," a phrase that pinpoints the permissive yet strong gesture of the Stern poem. It might be called negative will, that is, willing oneself to lose control, to give oneself over to transformation. It is when the speaker stops holding on that he is reborn. The obsessive downward movement is reversed and the speaker becomes a risen god in the paradise of this world: "and I rise up, one more time in the brilliant sunlight . . . king of the water, / lord of the greasy log, lord of the lake." This tragi-comic version of death and apotheosis is a typical mythicization of mundane experience, in this case a swim in the river.

"In These Shadows" (*RC* 74) is another short but complex drama of falling and rising, death and metamorphosis. In this case, these are seen in connection with the quandary of knowledge or consciousness. The speaker begins by summarizing what he knows: "All that I know" about "the rose," "the paper snowflake," and "the living goddess." The rose is nature, the paper snowflake is art, and the living goddess is myth incarnate, a woman of "violent anger" seen occasionally in Stern. She is the angel of "The Expulsion" (*PP* 81–83) and is also "My Favorite Demon" (*L* 47). She probably stems from a real woman or series of women, but as usual in Stern, autobiography is not the point.

"In These Shadows" depicts death as a passage wherein knowledge is not exactly lost, but takes a different form; it is *altered* and pain becomes a shadow:

> All that I ever learned
> is suddenly altered
> and all the cunning and pain is reduced
> to a dark image where the body falls.

Altered may have been chosen to create the sound pattern, *all, altered, all, fall,* which rolls the stanza down to a full stop on the key word *falls.* Nevertheless, this word and its companion, *reduced,* are significant in light of the fact that elsewhere Stern calls death "a change" (*L* 13).

A new stanza begins with the abrupt yet musical reversal of tone so common in Stern; it has the gestural feel of a turning, like that of the chorus in strophe-antistrophe. This one is so ostentatious it's a shock: who would dare to say, "Oh sweetness, sweetness"?

Oh sweetness, sweetness! I can walk the length
of my dying maple; I can live again
in its old arms; I can watch it reach
out to the river, or stand like the first man
for hours in the cold sun,
looking at the soft ice,
sliding over the leaves,
disappearing in the blue water.

When the body falls, it is reborn in a return to paradise, where the speaker shares the innocence of Adam before he fell into knowledge and knew the goddess. He is able to disappear in the water, to die or what amounts to the same thing, to lose consciousness.

The easeful disappearance—the movement from presence to absence—imagined here contrasts with a wish *not* to disappear seen often in Stern, as above in "Rotten Angel." He also presents two kinds of immersion, the one where the speaker struggles and gasps and this relaxed one, seen also above in "Leaving Another Kingdom." This last type is an epiphany achieved by going down; more often it is by rising that the speaker dissolves in an apprehension of absence. Both consciousness and the imaginative experience of its loss are represented in Stern's dramatic interpretation of experience. These alternatives are not mutually exclusive but interdependent. As the speaker puts it in an early river poem: "I am living in both places at once" (*R* 49).

A more recent paradigm of Stern's response to burial and rebirth is "It Was a Rising" (*L* 53). Here, the worms studied briefly above in "For Song" become the instigation of an unruly verbal adventure: "It was a rising that brought the worms. They came / when the bodies came, the air was muddy, it was / a small mistake, the fingers were gone, the lips / were eaten away—" Here he may have been thinking of the Diet of Worms as well as the association between worms and death.

He cuts off that familiar train of thought at the dash, as if determined to avoid its ugly implications, and launches instead into a spree of eccentric associations. The speaker declares that he loves worms. He describes the "bags on their backs" and their "pointed sticks." At this point, we begin to doubt his understanding of worm anatomy. He retreats from talk of their best-known diet, focusing instead on their ability to "clean the ground of fruit and bottles, /

paper and plastic." This lie adds to our confusion. Then, abruptly, he says, "I was a worm once," and finally unmasks the metaphor he's been using: "I wore / an olive uniform, my specialty was Luckies, / I speared them by threes, I hooked a bone to a cup, / I caught the silver foil." The worms he's been talking about are workers who police an area with pointed sticks, as Stern did during his time in the army. His love for worms is his affection for the proletariat. As this context develops, it becomes more probable that the poet was thinking of the Diet of Worms, since Luther's attack on authority led to the peasant uprisings. This opening passage, almost a third of the poem, isn't conceptually related to the rest. This incongruence can be seen as a failure or as a willingness to display what happened when the poem was written.

In one sense, turning the worms into workers is a way to avoid their more obvious connotations. But it's only a temporary stay. The poem finally goes back to the worms and starts over. The speaker states a series of points that move out from fact to thesis in what seems a determined effort to get things straight:

> The rain when it comes
> forces the worms to the surface; that is another
> rising but not as cataclysmic. Love
> of one thing for another brought them up,
> and love will bring them back. This is the flesh
> that dies and this is the flesh that lives. . . .

Not as cataclysmic as the unspecified rising in the opening line? Not as cataclysmic as the resurrection? The lines are stubborn and ambiguous. The mind scurries about, looking for coherence; the poem tells the reader that the effort toward meaning is important in itself. The general point, that love connects the living and the dead, is clear, but the reference is puzzling.

Inscrutable passages occur fairly often in Stern but tend to get bypassed in an analysis that focuses on themes. The text sometimes acts as if it were a coded document that refers to a hidden master text. One of Stern's sources for the concept of a secret text is, as I have already pointed out, the Jewish mystical tradition. He also admires Whitman for having "a secret text—I am tempted to say *the* secret text." For Stern, Whitman's poems are an allusion to that text and a metaphoric rendering of it, even a series of riddles. The whole truth he kept to himself and released a little bit at a time. But then he lost or burned the text, good democrat that he was, a democrat and yet a priest, one of the very few. ("What Is This Poet?" 153)

In its secrecy, the Stern poem always, to one degree or another, urges the quest reading. The text challenges the questor to prove himself. It asks him to enact a process parallel to its own, to share the idiosyncratic associations of the poet's mind. As he does so, the reader is drawn to follow relationships not only in the single poem but also across the body of work. When this inherently egocentric kind of demand is taken to the extreme, as in *Finnegan's Wake*, the classic example, it severely limits the number of readers able to follow or willing to take the trouble. This of course creates a literati, a group of initiates privy to the "secret doctrine" of the work. In Stern's case, the goal is to make the poem widely available and mysterious at the same time. His poem is accessible first as an emotional encounter and next as a renewed enactment of universal symbols. Its fast-moving, pleasureful surface tends to disguise its underlying complexity.

"It Was a Rising" soon turns to the familiar Sternian drama of death and rebirth, recapitulating motifs used throughout the canon. The speaker lies "in coldness." He is buried in sand; he needs "a straw" to breathe through. He breaks free and rises; as usual he has a painful arm. He dives into the water, where he finds a "rolled-up scroll." Biblical scrolls, seen here and there in Stern, are tokens of the secret text. The speaker asserts that the scroll and the poem itself may be a "dream of Asbury Park" as a paradise "built on clouds" and held up by cherubs, one of the orders of angels. It may not be a dream, however; it may be "the city itself." The poem closes as the speaker pictures himself "with an unlined notebook, / ready for my own visionary window, / ready for a whole morning of sunlight and silence."[12]

"It Was a Rising" is an extreme example of Stern's conviction that his poem must reveal the speaker's struggle against a chaos of meanings and his effort to subdue death through verbal transformation. If, as Stern has suggested, he succeeds by failing—by virtue of his failure to exercise tight-fisted control over a poem's impulses, this poem is one of his notable successes.[13]

To recognize the extremity of its performance, one need only compare its brokenness, roughness, and veering possibilities with a poem of similar theme and method such as Frost's "Birches." Frost's master poem is also a performance of the mind in which a concrete image leads to considerations of death and rebirth. However, Frost's fear of disappearing, of rising and not coming back down, is stated:

> May no fate willfully misunderstand me
> And half grant what I wish and snatch me away
> Not to return. . . .

In spite of the dangerous direction taken in "Birches," the voice remains smooth and calm; the statement controls itself. Stern's poem is a further radicalization of the tendency toward performance seen in Frost. And its opening imagery of worms and half-eaten bodies, though comically odd, is brutal; it makes Frost's birches seem gentler and more comforting than they did before. "It Was a Rising" seems to be taking a dare.

Stern retreats from the edge of the precipice in his final lines, as if to say, "Look how far I can 'lean out' and still come back." The final section provides the recognition and confirmation of a familiar ritual recurrence; it intends to impose silence on contingency. Extremely random and illogical texts are often said, in what has become a critic's cliché, to represent meaninglessness. However, inclusion of the seemingly irrelevant or unintelligible in a poetic universe that is finally meaningful asserts that truth can accept, accommodate, or enfold disorder.

The Stern performance is a denial of Faustian limitations achieved through what Eliot termed the ultra-dramatic, "the speech of creatures who are more than human, or rather, seen in a light more than that of day" (Drew 127). In heroic times, poets were able to take lives of great significance for subjects: questors, princes, even Adam, even God himself. Today, the poet must find a way to cast his own life—his own speech—in "a light more than that of day." Many simply assume for their private lives an importance beyond itself. Some create significance through verbal brilliance or potent simplicity. Some try to preserve the innocence of events; others turn to the isolation of the impersonal language act. Stern chooses neither remote impersonality nor concentration on small moments of private significance. His response to the call for a hero is not to heroize his actual life but to reimagine himself as an exemplary figure, an ultraself, "a creature more than human." In the poem, he continually dies and is reborn as the artist-creator, the questor, the intermediary, and the prophet.

The central mission of this hero is to validate our habitation by recognizing in this world the ghost of another, the intimation of paradise. This paradise is not a proposition but a state of mind created or recovered fortuitously through a performance of the imagination. Stern describes it as a sabbatical vision: "On the Sabbath man is free from the chains of nature and from the chains of time, for there is no nature, and there is no time, although it is only for one day a week." The Sabbath is an act of "will and imagination" which encompasses "not only an anticipation of Messianic time but also a nostalgic reminder of Gardenic time." Reminders of it can be accomplished in the poem, which, like the Sabbath day, is a finite example, but it cannot be described: "Is it a state of non-existence, or is it a state of existence? Is consciousness intensified or is it obliterated? Is total consciousness, or total absorption, a form of obliteration?" Though the sabbatical vision cannot be defined, it is, he asserts, "the purpose of history, perhaps of existence" (Notes" 13.1: 17–18).

Stern's aesthetic invites criticism because it is traditional. It may be called yet another version of the lyrical ego, of Yeats's "cry of the heart." But our obsessive reverence for the new has led us to embrace much that is trivial. Seduced by the values of the culture at large, art has equated newness with merit and, conversely, familiarity with weakness. This adolescent overemphasis on continual revolution has led to the loss of most of the art audience and trivialized art itself. What we need to reject is not the central, timeless issues confronted in traditionl verse but their abuse in bad poetry. What we have come to dislike in the romantic lyric is not the quandary of consciousness or the quest for transcendence itself, but the facile sentiment, the smug certainty, the patronizing attitude of slick romanticism. The truth is, we hunger for a poetry both readable and substantial, a poetry that is brilliant and inventive but also human and profound. In Stern, we have a vision of scope and intensity able to revalidate the "cry of the heart."

Notes

Chapter I

1. Parenthetical abbreviations are used herein for Stern's books as follows: *Rejoicings*: R; *Lucky Life*: LL; *The Red Coal*: RC; *Paradise Poems*: PP; *Lovesick*: L.

2. The Pine Barrens continues to be a valuable symbolic territory in later Stern. See my discussion of "For Night to Come" in chapter III.

3. *The Naming of Beasts*, published in 1972 by Cummington Press, is identical in content, except that *Rejoicings* contains one additional poem.

4. Personal interview, March 17, 1988.

Chapter II

1. When Coleridge defined the organic poem, he called it innate and opposed it to the mechanical, but his meaning has since slipped.

2. The use of "explaining him" instead of "explaining to him" (the spirit of America) is a Pittsburgh colloquialism. Personal interview, July 1, 1988.

3. Stern lived in Philadelphia from 1956 to 1963 and has been in Iowa City from fall 1982 through the present.

4. I am indebted to Rob Wilson, who suggested the phrases "surrealism of wit" and "zany flux of rhetoric."

Chapter III

1. The Marlborough Blenheim is the hotel which is seen being blown up in the opening sequence of the film *Atlantic City*.

2. These figures, known as Vitruvian man, also contained a square; the best known example is that of Leonardo.

3. An allusion to the "great violence" of the destruction of Jerusalem and the dispersal of the Jews.

4. Personal interview, July 2, 1988.

5. For a discussion of these perspectives in Clemens, see Marx 20–26.

6. Stern's first book-length publication, a long poem called "The Pineys," deals with this place and its people. See chapter I.

7. Personal interview, July 1, 1988.

8. The windowsill garden was in the kitchen at 718 N. Gilbert Street, Iowa City, where Stern lived during spring and summer of 1985 and 1986. "Grapefruit" and a number of other poems were also written here.

9. The "slogans and brown faces," as well as the words "Plaza Caribe," were painted on the wall of a building edging the people's garden. Telephone interview, May 24, 1988.

10. Weeds are also identified with the "sprouts" in the Zohar; the Shekinah (Malkhut) grows "sprouts of secrets": new interpretations of Torah.

11. Personal interview, March 16, 1988.

12. Personal interview, March 17, 1988.

Chapter IV

1. Personal interview, July 1, 1988. The Midrashim are commentaries on the Hebrew scriptures written between A.D. 100 and 1200; they have recently become models for a literary criticism of appropriation.

2. Telephone interview, March 20, 1988.

3. I am grateful to Michael Cooke for his comments on the trope of the stranger.

4. See chapter III.

5. Personal interview, July 1, 1988.

6. Stern saw the film in 1979, in the former Van Dam Theater, on Van Dam Street near Sixth Avenue.

7. A garland is also an anthology of poetry.

8. Personal interview, July 1, 1988.

9. Frederick Garber suggests that *clawing* provides a glimpse of dark places in the self "whose urgencies for their own solution propel them upward" (45).

10. Phone interview, May 1, 1988; personal interview, July 1, 1988; phone interview, September 3, 1988.

11. Stern identifies the Jew as "a holder of strange credentials" in an earlier poem, "Peace in the Near East" (*LL* 31). The "bills of lading" in "Stolen Face" recall Eliot's Tiresias. In his role as Mr. Eugenides, he carries "documents" identified by Eliot in a note as "the Bill of Lading etc" ("The Fire Sermon," *The Waste Land*).

12. Phone interview, September 3, 1988.

Chapter V

1. The Greek *angelos*, from an unknown Oriental source, also means *messenger*.

2. In cases where ordinary deeds were originally accomplished by God himself, the word *angel* was inserted later because the concept of God became too exalted for such earthly matters.

3. See chapter III.

4. See chapter I.

5. Mythical giants are one of the sources of angels; their great height is emphasized in the haggadic literature, where they are sometimes as tall as the world itself.

6. The "dancing whale" was a sign on top of the Hotel Imperial.

7. In Jacob's dream, as recorded in the Elohist or so-called E Code of the Hexateuch, dated in the eighth to seventh centuries B.C. The ladder also refers to the "rungs" in Hassidic literature.

8. Stern lived in Raubsville from 1969 through 1982, his longest period of residence in one place as an adult.

9. Personal interview, July 1, 1988. The names of angels were constructed by attaching *mal'ach* as a prefix to another term.

10. The picture of Yahweh in Isaiah 6, which takes most of its detail from a Babylonian source. Yahweh is seen as a throned, solar deity, surrounded by seraphim.

11. The "fat girl" may be an allusion to Stevens's "fat girl, terrestrial, my summer, my night," in "Notes toward a Supreme Fiction."

12. This "visionary window" was actually that of a Perkins Pancake House on the boardwalk in Ocean Grove, New Jersey. Phone interview, September 10, 1988.

13. See chapter IV.

Works Cited

Primary Sources

Glaser, Elton, ed. "Gerald Stern Speaking." *Akros* 8–9 (1984): 5–30. Edited and rearranged comments made in answer to questions from students at Akron University.

Hillringhouse, Mark. "Gerald Stern: Ten Poems and an Interview." *American Poetry Review* 13.2 (1984): 19–30. The interview took place in April 1982.

Pinsker, Sanford. "The Poetry of Constant Renewal and Celebration: An Afternoon's Chat with Gerald Stern." *Missouri Review* 4.2 (1980): 55–67. Reprinted in Pinsker, *Conversations with Contemporary American Writers*, Amsterdam: Costerus, 1985, 84–95.

Stern, Gerald. "Father Guzman." *Paris Review* 83 (1982): 41–81.

———. "A Few Words on Form." *Poetry East* 20–21 (1986): 146–50.

———. "For Night to Come." *45 Contemporary Poems*. New York: Longman, 1985, 213–18. Poem, editorial comment, and comment by Gerald Stern.

———. "Life Is Not a River: Some Thoughts on Teaching Poetry." *AWP Newsletter* 20.2 (1987): 6–9.

———. *Lovesick*. New York: Harper & Row, 1987.

———. *Lucky Life*. Boston: Houghton Mifflin, 1977.

———. "Notes from the River." Column. *American Poetry Review* 12.1 (1983): 20–22 [on ruins]; 12.3 (1983): 42–44 [on pockets]; 12.5 (1983): 36–38 [on nostalgia]; 13.1 (1984): 17–19 [on the sabbath]; 16.3 (1987): 41–46 [on caves].

———. *Paradise Poems*. New York: Random House, 1984.

———. "The Pineys." *Journal of the Rutgers University Library* 32.2 (1969): 55–80.

———. *The Red Coal*. Boston: Houghton Mifflin, 1981.

———. *Rejoicings*. Los Angeles: Metro Book Company, 1984. First published in 1973.

———. "Some Secrets." *In Praise of What Persists*. Ed. Stephen Berg. New York: Harper & Row, 1983, 255–65.

———. "'Sycamore': Poem and Commentary." *Poesis* 5.4 (1984): 1–11.

———. "What Is This Poet?" *What Is a Poet?* Ed. Hank Lazar. Tuscaloosa: University of Alabama Press, 1987, 145–56.

Secondary Sources

Bachelard, Gaston. *The Poetics of Reverie*. Boston: Beacon Press, 1960.

Barthes, Roland. Trans. Richard Miller. *The Pleasure of the Text*. Trans. Richard Miller. New York: Hill and Wang–Farrar Straus, 1975.

———. *S/Z*. Trans. Richard Miller. New York: Hill and Wang, 1974.

———. "To Write: An Intransitive Verb?" *The Structuralist Controversy: The Language of Criticism and the Sciences of Man*. Ed. Richard Macksey and Eugenio Donato. Baltimore: Johns Hopkins University Press, 1970, 134–56.

Beja, Morris. *Epiphany in the Modern Novel*. Seattle: University of Washington Press, 1971.

Bellow, Saul. *Henderson the Rain King*. Greenwich, Conn.: Fawcett Crest, 1959.

Benamou, Michel. "Presence and Play." *Performance in Postmodern Culture*. Ed. Michel Benamou and Charles Caramello. Madison, Wis.: Coda Press, 1977, 3–7.

Bly, Robert. "Recognizing the Image as a Form of Intelligence." *Field* 24 (1891): 17–27.

Broyard, Anatole. "Love, Nostalgia and Niagara." *New York Times Book Review*, February 16, 1986, 11.

Bruns, Gerald L. "Cain: Or, The Metaphorical Construction of Cities." *Salmagundi* 74–75 (1987): 70–85.

De Man, Paul. *Blindness and Insight: Essays in the Rhetoric of Contemporary Criticism*. Minneapolis: University of Minneapolis Press, 1971.

Drew, Elizabeth. *T. S. Eliot: The Design of His Poetry*. New York: Scribner's, 1949.

Garber, Frederick. "Pockets of Secrecy, Places of Occasion: On Gerald Stern." *American Poetry Review* 15.4 (1986): 38–47.

Heaney, Seamus. "Place, Pastness, Poems: A Triptych." *Salmagundi* 68–69 (1985–86): 30–47. Special issue: "The Literary Imagination and the Sense of the Past."

Hoover, Paul. "Moral Poetry." *American Book Review* 7.1 (1985): 14–15.

Langer, Susanne. *Feeling and Form*. New York: Scribner's, 1953.

Marx, Leo. *The Machine in the Garden: Technology and the Pastoral Ideal in America*. New York: Oxford University Press, 1964.

Merwin, W. S. *Green with Beasts*. New York: Knopf, 1956.

Nietzsche, Friedrich. *The Birth of Tragedy*. Trans. Francis Golffing. Garden City, N.Y.: Doubleday Anchor, 1956.

Palmer, Richard. "Toward a Postmodern Hermeneutics of Performance." *Performance in Postmodern Culture*. Ed. Michel Benamou and Charles Caramello. Madison, Wis.: Coda Press, 1977, 19–31.

Paz, Octavio. *Children of the Mire: Modern Poetry from Romanticism to the Avant-Garde*. Cambridge: Harvard University Press, 1974.

Perl, Jeffrey M. *The Tradition of Return: The Implicit History of Modern Literature*. Princeton: Princeton University Press, 1984.

Pinsky, Robert. *The Situation of Poetry: Contemporary Poetry and Its Traditions*. Princeton: Princeton University Press, 1976.

Quinones, Ricardo J. *Mapping Literary Modernism: Time and Development*. Princeton: Princeton University Press, 1985.

Simpson, Louis. "Facts and Poetry." *Gettysburg Review* 1.1 (1988): 156–65. Includes a review of *Lovesick*.

Stitt, Peter. "Engagements with Reality." *Georgia Review* 35.4 (1981): 874–82. Includes a review of *The Red Coal*.

Turner, Alberta, ed. *45 Contemporary Poems*. New York: Longman, 1985. Editorial comment on "For Night to Come."

———. "Poetry 1981: Three Review Essays." *Field* 26 (1982): 68–76. Includes a review of *The Red Coal*.

Wright, James. *The Branch Will Not Break*. Middletown, Conn.: Wesleyan University Press, 1962.

Index

135

Index

Romanticism, 33, 56, 103, 127; and embrace of primitivity, 38; idealized perspective, 65; and imagery, 59, 71; and irony, 23; and irrelevance, 72; neo-, 24, 33; slick, 127. *See also* Paradox of consciousness
"Rose Warehouse, The," 62
"Rotten Angel," 118–19, 122, 123

Sabbath, 127
Secrecy, 26–28, 76, 103, 124-25; opposition between hidden and open, 93–94; secret agenda, 97; secret doctrine, 83, 124–25; secret enclosures, 93; secret metaphor, 82, 84; secret oral tradition, 83, 98, 99; secret steps and gestures, 98; the secret text, 94, 99, 124–25; and undertext, 84. *See also* Kabbala
Secret Text. *See* Emerson, Ralph Waldo; Kabbala; Secrecy
"Self Portrait," 99–100
"Sensitive Knife, The," 120
Simpson, Louis: review of *Lovesick*, 14–15
Sincere poem, the, 22, 24
Social poetry, 46–48
Stafford, William, 22, 45
"Steve Dunn's Spider," 121–22
Stevens, Wallace, 14, 17, 18, 32, 55, 72, 109, 130 n. 11 (ch. V)
"Stolen Face," 104–5
Structuralism, 14, 29
Suffering, 25, 34–35, 36, 56, 82, 115, 120; and the angel figure, 111; beauty out of, 117; imaginative transformation of, 12, 26, 117; and Jesus, 103; and pain, 111–13, 115; source of transcendence, 121
"Sycamore," 86–87, 106–8

Tammuz. *See* Bible
"Tashlikh," 102
"There Is Wind, There Are Matches," 92–93
"There I Was One Day," 89–90
"These Birds," 113
"This Is It," 92
"Three Skies," 52–55
Tragi-comedy, 33–36
Transcendence, 34, 53–56, 112, 121–22, 127; apotheosis, 122; the furthest limit, 122; "lightness," 52–53; radiant experience, 50; a second existence, 40; upwards fall, 53–54. *See also* Epiphany; Mythic time; Rebirth
Turner, Alberta: on "For Night to Come," 65
"Two American Haikus," 21
"Two Trees," 62

Whitman, Walt, 14, 17–18, 24, 32, 72, 124–25; *Leaves of Grass*, 14
Williams, William Carlos, 17, 18, 82
Wilson, Rob, 128 n. 4 (ch. II)
Wright, James, 45

Zen Buddhism, 84, 88, 102, 104, 120

Jane Somerville is a poet-critic whose essays and poetry have appeared in *American Poetry Review, Gettysburg Review, Ohio Review*, and other journals. A recipient of several NEH grants, she is a professor of English at West Virginia University–Parkersburg, where she teaches creative writing and American literature. This is her first book-length critical study.

The manuscript was edited by Lee Ann Schreiner.
The book was designed by Mary Krzewinski.
The typeface for the display is Delphin No. 2.
The typeface for the text is Palatino.

The book is printed on 55-lb. Glatfelter paper and is bound in Roxite A-Grade cloth.

Manufactured in the United States of America.